AID FOR TRADE
IN ASIA AND THE PACIFIC
NAVIGATING CLIMATE POLICY DYNAMICS
FOR SUSTAINABLE TRADE COMPETITIVENESS

JUNE 2024

ASIAN DEVELOPMENT BANK

ADB

© 2024 Asian Development Bank
6 ADB Avenue, Mandaluyong City, 1550 Metro Manila, Philippines
Tel +63 2 8632 4444; Fax +63 2 8636 2444
www.adb.org

Some rights reserved. Published in 2024.

ISBN 978-92-9270-782-8 (print); 978-92-9270-783-5 (PDF); 978-92-9270-784-2 (ebook)
Publication Stock No. TCS240333-2
DOI: http://dx.doi.org/10.22617/TCS240333-2

This publication has been co-funded by the Asian Development Bank's (ADB) Technical Assistance Special Fund and the Australian Government through the Department of Foreign Affairs and Trade. The views expressed in this publication are those of the authors and do not necessarily reflect the views and policies of the ADB or its Board of Governors or the governments they represent, and of the Australian Government. The Australian Government neither endorses the views in this publication, nor vouches for the accuracy or completeness of the information contained within the publication. The Australian Government, its officers, employees and agents, accept no liability for any loss, damage or expense arising out of or in connection with any reliance on any omissions or inaccuracies in the material contained in this publication.

ADB does not guarantee the accuracy of the data included in this publication and accepts no responsibility for any consequence of their use. The mention of specific companies or products of manufacturers does not imply that they are endorsed or recommended by ADB in preference to others of a similar nature that are not mentioned.

By making any designation of or reference to a particular territory or geographic area in this document, ADB does not intend to make any judgments as to the legal or other status of any territory or area.

Corrigenda to ADB publications may be found at http://www.adb.org/publications/corrigenda.

Notes:
In this publication, "$" refers to United States dollars.
ADB recognizes "China" as the People's Republic of China, "Vietnam" as Viet Nam, and "Russia" as the Russian Federation.

Cover design by Mike Cortes.

Contents

PART 1

PART 2

Tables, Figures, and Boxes

Boxes

Foreword

The 2024 Global Aid for Trade Review comes at a time when every stakeholder in the global trading system must recognize the many and varied challenges to an open and free global trading system that promotes equitable and sustainable development. The coronavirus disease (COVID-19) pandemic reminded the world just how vulnerable markets are to exogenous shocks. As much as we may now celebrate the relatively robust economic recovery from the pandemic—a fact clearly evidenced in the trade data reviewed here—the crisis in public health nonetheless prompted policymakers to pay greater attention to supply chain risks for essential products.

There is a danger that concerns over access to essential goods may accelerate the trend toward fragmentation and away from nondiscriminatory trade liberalization. The pandemic aftermath has seen rising demands for localized supply chains and subsidies and preferences for local production. While serving national policy objectives, these trends could prove quite costly to developing countries, both in the Asia and Pacific region and elsewhere, that view access to foreign markets as critical for economic growth and raising standards of living.

The links between climate change and trade, the principal focus of the present report, challenges the world to find the will to continue to act collectively. There has perhaps never been such a truly global challenge given that climate change respects no national borders. Leaders have recognized for decades that temperatures are rising, that this trend is caused by human actions, and that meeting the challenge requires worldwide efforts to limit the emission of greenhouse gases.

Asian economies simultaneously face multiple risks. Many are highly susceptible to negative economic consequences of climate change, but rely more on carbon-intensive energy sources which makes their access to foreign markets more at risk if confronted with barriers to trade in high-carbon goods. Although economies in Asia and the Pacific generally are net exporters of carbon dioxide emissions, the region at the same time has achieved significant declines in the carbon intensity of production.

The different pace and depth of carbon pricing policies across the globe and their potential impact on trade competitiveness has provided an impetus for some countries to explore border adjustment mechanisms. Unilateral measures such as the European Union's Carbon Border Adjustment Mechanism (CBAM), which imposes fees on imported cement, iron and steel, aluminum, fertilizers, electricity, and hydrogen production, are intended to reduce leakage caused by shifting production to pollution havens that do not penalize "dirty" production. CBAM is still being phased in, so its actual effects remain speculative, but its tracing and reporting requirements will certainly increase compliance costs. Research summarized here shows that investments in green technologies can help mitigate the negative trade effects estimated for all countries and regions.

The links between trade and climate change offer opportunities as well as challenges. Trade in environmental goods and services provides significant positive externalities, helping countries cope with climate change. It can facilitate the advancement, availability, and utilization of environmental technologies, helping to mitigate emissions by stimulating innovation and driving down the costs of low-carbon technologies. Asia and the Pacific enjoys a substantial trade surplus in environmental goods, although trade in such goods is highly concentrated, with relatively few countries accounting for most of the trade.

The greening of Aid for Trade requires a concerted effort to incorporate climate considerations into trade-related legislation and regulations. The report demonstrates the need to support economies in enhancing their policy frameworks to respond to external challenges posed by barriers to trade in environmental goods, and to harness green technologies and industries for growth and development. Aid for Trade is well placed to play a valuable coordinating role, providing financing for the energy transition in tradable sectors.

Albert F. Park
Chief Economist and Director General
Economic Research and Development Impact Department
Asian Development Bank

Acknowledgments

This report was prepared by the Regional Cooperation and Integration Division (ERCI) of the Asian Development Bank (ADB) Economic Research and Development Impact Department under RETA-10242: Aid for Trade for Inclusive Growth, 2023–2025 (Subproject 3) financed by ADB's Technical Assistance Special Fund and by the Department of Foreign Affairs and Trade (DFAT), Government of Australia.

ERCI Director Jong Woo Kang provided overall direction and supervision of the report. The main contributors of the report are Pramila Crivelli, Neil Foster-McGregor, and Craig VanGrasstek.

Background papers were prepared by Prachi Agarwal, Neil Foster-McGregor, Joe Francois, Michael Jakob, Jodie Keane, Önder Nomaler, Håkan Nordström, Bart Verspagen, and Hauke Ward. The report also benefited from contributions from Komal Biswal, Sajid Ghani, Gerald Pascua, Kenji Takamiya, and Mara Tayag. Comments and inputs from DFAT are also acknowledged.

Pramila Crivelli and Paulo Rodelio Halili coordinated the production of this report with administrative support from Amiel Bryan Esperanza.

Craig VanGrasstek edited the manuscript. Mike Cortes created the cover design and typeset the figures and tables. Joe Mark Ganaban did the layout and typesetting of the report. Tuesday Soriano performed proofreading, while Marjorie Celis did the page proof checking, with support from Paulo Rodelio Halili and Carol Ongchangco. Support for printing and publishing this report was provided by the Printing Services Unit of ADB's Corporate Services Department and by the publishing team of the Department of Communications and Knowledge Management.

Abbreviations

ADB	Asian Development Bank
AfT	Aid for Trade
APEC	Asia-Pacific Economic Cooperation
ASEAN	Association of Southeast Asian Nations
BCA	border carbon adjustment
CAGR	compound annual growth rates
CBAM	Carbon Border Adjustment Mechanism
CGE	computable general equilibrium
CLEG	Combined List of Environmental Goods
CO_2	carbon dioxide
COVID-19	coronavirus disease
CPC	Central Product Classification
CPTPP	Comprehensive and Progressive Agreement for Trans-Pacific Partnership
CSDDD	Corporate Sustainability Due Diligence Directive
DMC	developing member country
DPP	Dialogue on Plastics Pollution
DTIS	diagnostic trade integration study
EG	environmental goods
EGS	environmental goods and services
EIF	Enhanced Integrated Framework
ETS	Emissions Trading Scheme
EU	European Union
FDI	foreign direct investment
FFSR	Fossil Fuel Subsidy Reform
FIT	feed-in tariff
FTA	free trade agreement
GDP	gross domestic product
GEA	Green Economy Agreement
GHG	greenhouse gas
GVC	global value chain
IPR	intellectual property right
Lao PDR	Lao People's Democratic Republic
LDC	least developed country
LLDC	landlocked developing country

MSMEs	micro, small, and medium-sized enterprises
MTS	multilateral trading system
NAPA	National Adaptation Programmes of Action
NDC	nationally determined contribution
ODA	official development assistance
OECD	Organisation for Economic Co-operation and Development
PRC	People's Republic of China
PPP	public-private partnership
PV	photovoltaic
R&D	research and development
RCEP	Regional Comprehensive Economic Partnership
RTA	regional trade agreement
SDG	Sustainable Development Goal
SIDS	small island developing states
SMEs	small and medium-sized enterprises
TESSD	Trade and Environmental Sustainability Structure Discussions
UNFCCC	United Nations Framework Convention on Climate Change
WTO	World Trade Organization

Executive Summary

Part 1 reviews the broader trends for trade and development in Asia and the Pacific. The region's share of global trade has been on an upward trajectory for decades, and—notwithstanding shifts and interruptions—that rise continues unabated. While it will take greater historical perspective before one may say so definitively, there is good reason to believe that, from a purely economic perspective, the recent emergency in global public health was a short-term deviation from long-established trends rather than a major inflection point.

When seen in a larger context, however, the short-term economic effects of the coronavirus disease (COVID-19) pandemic on the movement of goods, services, and capital may be less significant than the way that this emergency reinforced longer-term trends in the perceptions and actions of policymakers. It offered a reminder of how vulnerable the world is to exogenous shocks, reinforcing the demands in some economies to localize supply chains for goods that are perceived to be of essential utility. This development could harm the economic interests of the poorest economies, especially if it exacerbates the pattern by which major economies put local production and "friend-shoring" ahead of nondiscriminatory trade liberalization. It may also contribute to a trend discussed in Part 2, whereby major economies adjust their trade policies to accommodate local demands in other areas of public policy. The final results will depend in part on how well this region and its partners deal with other global challenges. It is in that context that the debate over climate change offers an opportunity for the world either to exacerbate or reverse what looks like a slide away from globalization and cooperation.

Several observations stand out regarding trade growth for the Asia and Pacific region since 2005:

- For the region as a whole, the rates of growth for exports are almost identical to those for imports, both in goods and in services.

- Trade in services has expanded at a faster pace than has trade in goods.

- Developing Asia, and especially least developed countries (LDCs), experienced substantially faster trade expansion than the advanced economies in the region.

- Trade expansion has been relatively rapid for all of the developing subregions, with the Central Asian subregion being the only one with below-average growth for goods as well as services.

The report reviews trends in the region's imports and exports of environmental goods and services (EGS). Asia and the Pacific enjoys a substantial trade surplus in environmental goods, with its collective exports to the world being two-thirds larger than its imports in 2022. The data also show a high concentration of trade in this sector, with relatively small numbers of economies accounting for most of the trade and only half a dozen being net exporters. Total Asia and Pacific environmental goods (EG) imports rose over the period of 2007–2022, yet a few downturns punctuated the generally upward pattern.

Aid for Trade (AfT) disbursements in Asia and the Pacific are recuperating. The Asia and Pacific share was 33.6% in 2020–2022, down from 35.0% in 2017–2019. The relative importance varies by subregion, with AfT representing more than half of total official development assistance disbursements received by India, and also for large shares for Bangladesh, several economies in Southeast Asia and Central Asia, as well as Palau in the Pacific. The LDCs constitute a special group among the developing economies. Eight of the ten remaining LDCs in the region are either landlocked developing countries (LLDC) or small island developing states (SIDS); AfT is especially important for the LDCs in that latter category.

Part 2 explores how the Asia and Pacific region can best maintain trade competitiveness while navigating the dynamics of climate policy. It is founded on the premise that a shift toward a low-carbon economy could be bolstered by ambitious, credible, and timely climate policies. Trade can be a part of the solution when globalization allows the production of energy-intensive goods in locations with the best low-carbon energy potentials, enables new technologies, and synergizes multinational efforts to reduce carbon emissions. Measures to alleviate uncertainty in low-carbon investments are imperative, especially through quality infrastructure, yet policies should also be based upon an equitable sharing of the burdens and be politically sustainable.

A global response to climate change is made more difficult by the asymmetric distribution of the costs associated with both action and inaction. The Asia and Pacific region is a net exporter of carbon emissions, and economies are at risk from more than one direction. Some are especially susceptible to climate-change damage, they are less carbon-competitive than more developed regions, and their access to extra-regional markets may be jeopardized by border barriers to high-carbon goods. Developing economies have lately overtaken the developed as carbon dioxide emitters. Yet, the Asia and Pacific region has achieved significant declines in carbon intensity. Most of the region's larger economies had the greatest declines in carbon intensity, putting them as well as SIDS in a better position to handle these threats to their competitiveness than are their poorer neighbors. Those economies that still have above-average carbon intensities are most exposed to the impacts of ambitious climate targets.

Aid for Trade's goal of assisting the integration of developing economies into the multilateral trading system, and with the simultaneous demand to address climate change, need not be seen as mutually exclusive objectives. Environmental sustainability has emerged as a pivotal aspect of trade policy for predicating climate-resilient pathways and propelling the global economy toward a greener trajectory. When economies integrate environmental considerations in AfT activities, they enhance their adaptation and resilience to climate change, facilitating a sustainable recovery and promoting export diversification and competitiveness.

The greening of AfT entails the mainstreaming of climate within the project, reflecting a concerted effort to incorporate climate considerations into trade-related legislation and regulations. Sustainability criteria are now being embedded into the policy analysis and implementation of regional trade agreement, for example, and multilateral agreements are dealing with the climate implication of technical barriers to trade, sanitary and phytosanitary standards, and other topics. AfT helps to harmonize trade-related climate standards and streamline customs procedures for environmentally friendly goods and technologies, aiming to improve import and export procedures for sustainable products and to promote green trade. AfT also helps to train trade officials, business leaders, and other stakeholders to sensitize them on the importance of integrating a climate agenda for sustainability, and helps build productive capacity through novel interventions. AfT support for cleaner energy production complements trade policies that facilitate access to new technologies and standards compliance.

Climate change has been a leading issue in the international community for the past generation. Nearly all countries have Paris Agreement commitments, and the issue is also deliberated in other regional, plurilateral, and multilateral settings. Engaging in high-quality trade agreements can support the global transition through enhanced market access and more diversified EGS trade. If supported by appropriate government interventions and regulations, diversifying trade and investment can promote access to less resource-intensive, environment-friendly products, thereby inducing the shift to less pollution-driven production methods.

EGS trade offers significant positive externalities, helping economies better cope with the effects of climate change and the policy responses of their foreign partners. Trade can facilitate the advancement, availability, and utilization of environmental technologies, thus mitigating greenhouse gas emissions by stimulating innovation and driving down the costs of low-carbon technologies through efficiency and economies of scale. EGS trade also allows economies to adapt environmental technologies to their local requirements. Progress to liberalize trade in environmental goods and services has been modest. The Asia and Pacific region's average tariffs on environmental goods imports from the world are only slightly lower than the tariffs on all imports, and regional preferences in this sector are slight. Trade in environmental services has been given even less attention compared to trade in goods.

New generation trade agreements such as the Regional Comprehensive Economic Partnership Agreement (RCEP) may achieve some further liberalization and expansion of EGS trade. Data associate the presence of a trade agreement with a 5.5% increase in global value chain trade, and such agreements can also produce positive environmental results. Research reviewed here shows that the presence of an environmental provision in a trade agreement is associated with reduced embodied emissions trade of around 4.1%, and that these effects are greater still for low-income exporters where an environmental provision is estimated to reduce embodied emissions by 16.3%. Innovative initiatives such as the Singapore–Australia Green Economy Agreement (GEA) and the Asia-Pacific Economic Cooperation's EGS reference list also help promote environmental goods and services trade in support of positive environmental outcomes.

One major divide concerns the use of unilateral measures such as border carbon adjustments (BCAs). Although the issue has not made it onto the agenda in environmental conferences, despite the best efforts of some developing economies, larger economies are moving ahead unilaterally. By taxing imports based on their emissions content, BCAs are intended to reduce the risk of "carbon leakage," where carbon-intensive production is moved abroad to take advantage of lax standards, or, for example, where steel that might otherwise have been sourced locally will be imported from economies not subject to the same carbon pricing. In doing so, BCAs can mitigate the pollution haven hypothesis, and level the playing field for economies with higher carbon prices, which put their domestic producers at a competitive disadvantage due to the costs of complying with environmental regulations.

The European Union's (EU) Carbon Border Adjustment Mechanism (CBAM) is the first BCA of its kind. CBAM will initially cover cement, iron and steel, aluminum, fertilizers, electricity, and hydrogen production. As it is still being phased in, the actual effects remain speculative. At a minimum, it increases compliance costs by requiring exporters to file statements that had not previously been required. Research summarized here further suggests real costs for the Asia and Pacific economies, especially those where the affected products figure prominently in their exports. A computable general equilibrium model estimates that the trade effects will be negative for all economies and regions. Nor is CBAM the only EU instrument that seeks to complement local environmental rules with border measures. The interests of the Asia and Pacific exporters may also be impacted by the European Union Deforestation Regulation, as well as its Corporate Sustainability Due Diligence Directive.

Green technologies offer part of the solution. One important subset of these technologies concerns the production of clean energy, where recent improvements have made them highly price-competitive relative to fossil fuels. The People's Republic of China (PRC) and Viet Nam are major suppliers of solar photovoltaic power generation technologies, for example, and other Mekong economies with significant solar power potential can learn from Viet Nam's success by focusing on reforming regulations and building capacity to enhance competitiveness. Green-technology innovation nevertheless tends to be especially concentrated in a small number of economies, with 93%–94% of global patents originating from just five economies (the PRC, Japan, the United States, the Republic of Korea, and Germany). For most other economies, gaining access to green technologies requires diffusion through trade and foreign direct investment.

Access to technologies is especially important for LDCs, as this offers a path for suppliers of raw materials to move up the value chain. If LDCs are left using outdated technologies, this will compound the challenge of export diversification and hinder the role of trade in supporting adaptation to climate change. Support for capacity-building and technical assistance will be crucial in enabling developing economies to enhance their capabilities in green technologies and allow them to benefit from imported green technologies, and develop as a destination for green foreign direct investments.

Chapter 8 offers conclusions and recommendations on how to translate climate challenges into Aid for Trade opportunities. The report demonstrates the need for AfT to support economies in enhancing their policy frameworks to face the external challenges posed by such mechanisms, and to harness green technologies and industries for growth and development.

With regard to the process of domestic policymaking, the coordination of trade and environmental policy requires close collaboration between ministries that have not traditionally cooperated closely. Positive steps would include the following:

1. *Develop integrated policy frameworks.* Such frameworks will help align national trade policies and objectives, with success depending on interministerial coordination. AfT can foster coordination to ensure environmental foresight in national trade strategies.

2. *Conduct interministerial policy development workshops and training programs.* Through training programs and other means, AfT can facilitate the integration of trade and environmental priorities into coherent strategies that reflect sustainable trade and environmental protection.

3. *Leverage technology and data-sharing between ministries.* Evidence-based policymaking is frustrated whenever data are either unavailable or not shared. A mechanism for the effective exchange of trade and climate data between ministries would improve policy-level outcomes.

4. *Harmonizing performance metrics.* Joint development of interministerial performance metrics would improve synergies by providing a tool to measure the impact of integrated policymaking.

5. *Creating an enabling domestic regulatory framework for the development of green sectors.* Domestic regulation frameworks such as investment and intellectual property policies can help facilitate technology development and diffusion while promoting local and foreign green investments.

With regard to the substance of trade and environmental policies, Aid for Trade is well placed to play a similar coordinating and networking role, but also providing financing for the energy transition in trade sectors. The minimal expectation is that problems of coherence will be avoided, so that climate and commerce are not seen to be at cross-purposes; a more ambitious goal is to promote those initiatives by which trade and the environment offer mutually reinforcing benefits. The following are among the recommendations for ways that AfT can support that larger objective:

- Fund ex ante impact assessments to determine where climate measures are required.

- Improve green-technology innovation to adapt existing technologies and develop new ones.

- Facilitate joint ventures, collaborative research and development, and technology collaboration programs.

- Establish carbon markets in developing economies through robust regulatory frameworks.

- Assess the benefits of integrating environmental sustainability in trade agreements.

- Provide grants, concessional loans, and subsidies to purchase energy-efficient machinery and technology.

- Offer market research and trade relationships for alternative markets or diversified product lines.

- Help economies meet CBAM requirements, and financially support CBAM-affected industries.

- Use BCA revenue to support sustainable development initiatives in exporting economies.

- Build capacity to implement effective emissions accounting and management systems.

- Focus disbursements on enhancing port facilities, roads, and logistical chains.

- Offer training programs, workshops, and seminars on the trade/climate links.

- Equip policymakers to integrate environmental considerations into trade policies effectively.

All of these steps can be complemented by suitable adjustments to the procedures by which global trade and environmental initiatives are pursued. To offer just one such example, national trade development strategies, diagnostic trade integration studies (DTIS), DTIS updates, or equivalent studies should refer to and draw on nationally determined contributions and National Adaptation Programmes of Action and integrate climate effects.

PART 1

Trade and Development in Asia and the Pacific

Chapter 1

Recent Trends in Asia and Pacific Trade

Trade remains indispensable in promoting economic growth and raising the standards of living for people in developing Asia.[1] While the predominant development model in this region is often characterized as "*export*-led growth," a closer look at actual trade patterns in the region demonstrates that it should be more broadly defined as "*trade*-led growth" in which imports are no less important than exports. This can be appreciated from the nearly identical appearances of Figures 1.1 and 1.2, which respectively show the evolution of the region's exports and imports

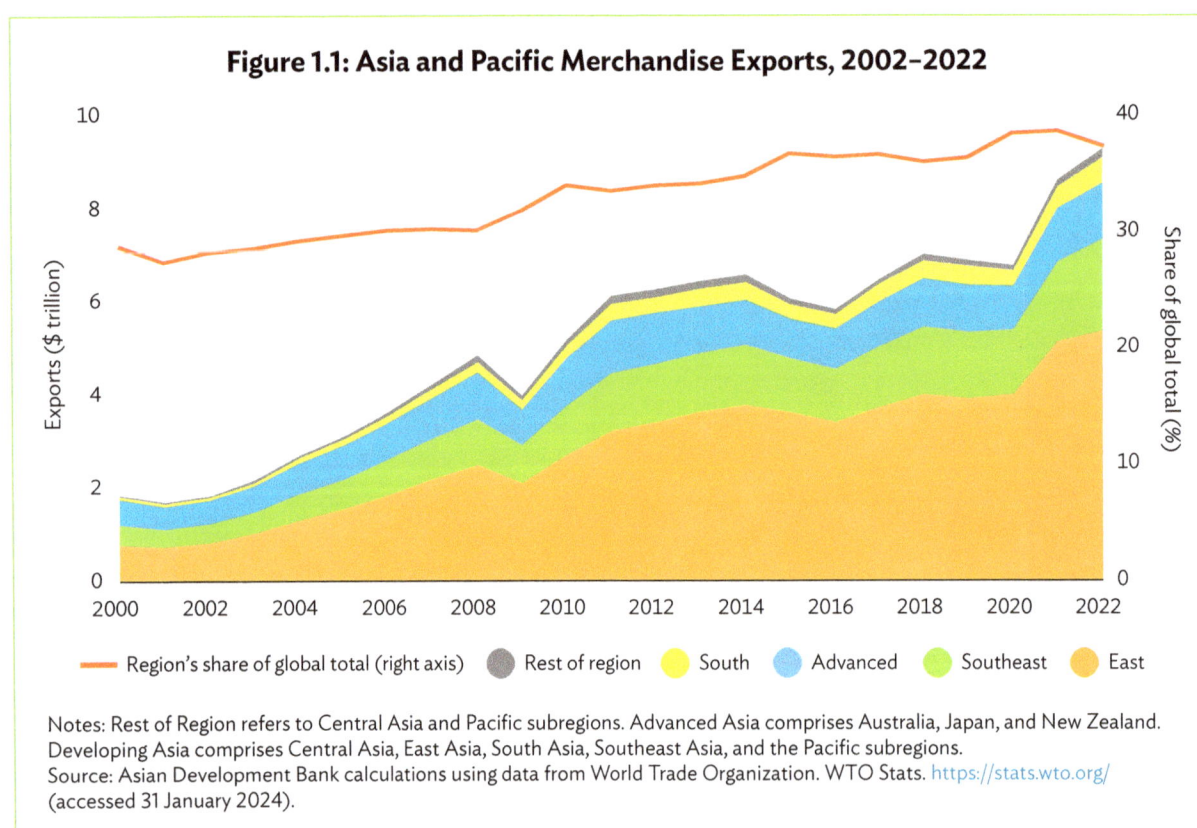

Figure 1.1: Asia and Pacific Merchandise Exports, 2002–2022

Notes: Rest of Region refers to Central Asia and Pacific subregions. Advanced Asia comprises Australia, Japan, and New Zealand. Developing Asia comprises Central Asia, East Asia, South Asia, Southeast Asia, and the Pacific subregions.
Source: Asian Development Bank calculations using data from World Trade Organization. WTO Stats. https://stats.wto.org/ (accessed 31 January 2024).

---

1   The term "developing Asia" refers to the 46 developing member economies of the Asian Development Bank (ADB). The developed economies refer to the economies of Australia, Japan, and New Zealand. Based on ADB's geographic operations, the 46 developing ADB member economies are divided into five subregions within the Asia and Pacific region. These subregions are Central and West Asia, East Asia, South Asia, Southeast Asia, and the Pacific.

Figure 1.2: Asia and Pacific Merchandise Imports, 2002–2022

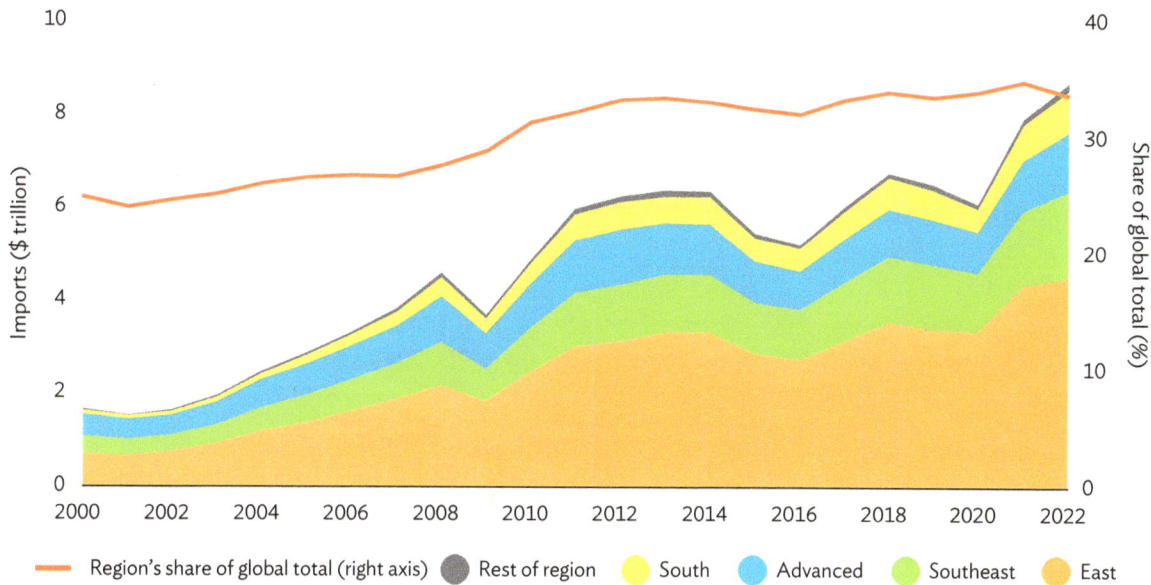

Notes: Rest of Region refers to Central Asia and Pacific subregions. Advanced Asia comprises Australia, Japan, and New Zealand. Developing Asia comprises Central Asia, East Asia, South Asia, Southeast Asia, and the Pacific subregions.
Source: Asian Development Bank calculations using data from World Trade Organization. WTO Stats. https://stats.wto.org/ (accessed 31 January 2024).

of goods since the turn of the century, reflecting the parallel development of global value chains (GVC). These data support the contention that expanded exports depend on expanded imports, with any rise or fall on one side of the ledger being closely tracked on the other.

The general trends over time have been for this region's share of global trade to rise, even while policymakers have devoted greater attention and resources to environmental needs. While the trends show continuity, the data also point to shifts and interruptions. Chief among the latter was the coronavirus disease (COVID-19) pandemic, which has had both short- and long-term effects on the cross-border movement of goods, services, and capital. We review those implications below, followed by analyses of Asia and Pacific trade in both goods and services generally and in those more pertinent to the environment.

The Short- and Long-Term Effects of the Pandemic

It has always been a challenge to balance the often-competing objectives of promoting trade and economic prosperity, achieving equity and development, and securing public health and environmental protection. The challenges became all the more acute when COVID-19, first discovered in 2019, became a global pandemic in 2020. Developing Asia's trade has now shown signs of a post-pandemic bounce back, yet there is also disparity in performance within the region.

Both the pandemic-induced downturns and the subsequent recoveries have been sharper for some subregions than others. On the export side in 2020, the results ranged from a sudden drop in Central Asia (down 20.4%) to a surprising (if modest) 2.3% expansion in East Asia. While exports rose in all subregions during 2021, the recovery was twice as high in South Asia (40.5%) as it was in the Pacific (19.6%). The data also put the impact of the pandemic in context, showing that while trade did contract for 2 successive years, the downturn was neither as prolonged as the one experienced during 2015–2016 nor nearly as sharp as the decline brought on by the Great Recession in 2009. Notwithstanding a small and possibly short-term contraction in 2022, the region held larger shares of global imports and exports that year (34.1% and 37.2%, respectively) than it had in either 2000 (25.3% and 28.6%) or in 2019 (34.0% and 36.2%). At the subregional level, East Asia continues to contribute the most to the region's merchandise trade, comprising 21.6% and 17.8% of global exports and imports in 2022, respectively. East Asia's export share in 2022 is a slight increase from 21% in 2019, while its import share is relatively unchanged. Merchandise trade export and import shares in 2022 for Southeast Asia (7.9% and 7.3%) and South Asia (2.2% and 3.6%) are higher compared to their respective 2019 shares. Central Asia's export share slightly increased from 0.6 in 2019 to 0.7 in 2022, while its imports share was unchanged at 0.5%. In contrast, the Pacific region's global exports and imports shares declined to 0.06% and 0.04% in 2022 from 0.07% and 0.05% in 2019.

While it will take greater historical perspective before we can say so definitively, there is good reason to believe that this emergency in global public health was a short-term deviation from long-established trends rather than a major inflection point. The pandemic was nevertheless a reminder of how vulnerable the world is to exogenous shocks. The same may be said for the pressing challenges brought by climate change, as well as technological disruptions. In each case, deep impacts on business and value chains accelerate the structural and digital trends that shape future economic growth. Beyond exposing widespread economic vulnerabilities, the pandemic also underscored the importance of innovative, resilient, and ecologically sustainable trade strategies.

The experience of many economies with the provision of critical goods and services has also propelled a post-pandemic trend by which economies seek to localize supply chains through trade restrictions on medical goods and other items perceived to be essential such as cereals, grains, fruits, and sugar (Asian Economic Integration Report 2023). This move could potentially harm economies that are least able to manufacture or provide these goods, similar to what happened during the pandemic. Current trends point to an increasing fragmentation of supply chains due to rising geopolitical tensions and future risk of escalation.

The rising concerns over security-of-supply coincide with, and could potentially exacerbate, a pre-pandemic trend that had already slowed further progress on nondiscriminatory trade liberalization. The founding of the World Trade Organization (WTO) in 1995 came at a time of high global confidence. That confidence is being increasingly tested in the face of geopolitical tensions, a progressive buildup of trade-restrictive measures and the resurgence of interest in the use of industrial policy. The members of this multilateral institution achieved substantial liberalization through the negotiation of free trade agreements (FTAs) and customs unions, which turned out to be highly beneficial for contracting parties.

It is possible that while the purely economic effects of the pandemic may already be largely behind us, its political implications may have greater staying power. To the extent that concerns over critical goods further encourage economies to stress "friend-shoring" over multilateralism, or to employ unilateral trade and investment measures that aim to promote local production and supply, future analysts may see COVID-19 as part of a historic turn away from globalization.

That trend is not inevitable, and will depend in part on how well this and other regions deal with other global challenges. As high as the stakes already are for environmental protection and climate change, they are made all the more important by the times in which this challenge arises. To the extent that economies can cooperate in addressing these global threats, and in devising a policy mix in which burdens are shared equitably and effectively, the issues discussed in Part 2 of this report offer an opportunity for economies to prove their capacity for collective action in pursuit of shared interests.

Overall Direction and Growth of Trade in Goods and Services

The larger trends can be appreciated from the data in Table 1.1, which summarizes the trajectory of Asia and Pacific trade in goods and services from 2005 through 2021 (for services) and 2022 (for goods). The overall pattern is one of strong growth in both imports and exports, and in services as well as goods, with the region experiencing compound annual growth rates (CAGRs) ranging from a respectable 5.55% (for merchandise exports) to an even more robust 6.33% (for services exports). Several observations stand out regarding trade growth since 2005:

- For the region as a whole, the rates of growth for exports are almost identical to those for imports, both in goods and in services.

- Trade in services has expanded at a somewhat faster pace than has trade in goods.

Table 1.1: Growth in Asia and Pacific Trade in Goods and Services, 2005–2021/2022
(3-year average values, $ billion and CAGR)

	Merchandise Exports			Merchandise Imports			Services Exports			Services Imports		
	2005–2007 ($)	2020–2022 ($)	CAGR (%)	2005–2007 ($)	2020–2022 ($)	CAGR (%)	2005–2007 ($)	2019–2021 ($)	CAGR (%)	2005–2007 ($)	2019–2021 ($)	CAGR (%)
Central	69.3	124.8	3.99	47.6	109.8	5.73	32.6	71.6	5.78	75.2	137.7	4.41
East	1,856.9	4,837.6	6.59	1,650.1	4,119.8	6.29	887.0	2,117.4	6.41	944.5	2,509.2	7.23
South	160.9	461.5	7.28	245.9	733.8	7.56	234.9	739.6	8.54	218.3	555.5	6.90
Southeast	763.8	1,690.3	5.44	688.6	1,591.1	5.74	499.5	1,347.7	7.35	547.3	1,438.1	7.14
Pacific	5.1	13.1	6.51	5.1	8.7	3.64	21.1	34.1	3.49	11.1	21.4	4.77
Advanced	799.3	1,093.6	2.11	743.5	1,075.0	2.49	571.8	998.4	4.06	708.9	1,247.6	4.12
Developing Asia	2,856.0	7,127.2	6.29	2,637.3	6,563.3	6.27	1,675.1	4,310.3	6.98	1,796.5	4,661.9	7.05
All of Asia and the Pacific	3,655.3	8,220.8	5.55	3,380.8	7,638.4	5.58	2,246.9	5,308.7	6.33	2,505.3	5,909.5	6.32

CAGR = compound annual growth rate, US = United States.
Notes: Data on services trade are not yet available for 2022. CAGR is calculated on the basis of 15 intervals for goods and 14 for services. Developing Asia refers to all of Asia and the Pacific other than the advanced economies.
Source: Asian Development Bank calculations using data from World Trade Organization. WTO Stats. https://stats.wto.org/ (accessed 31 January 2024).

■ Developing Asia, and especially least developed countries, experienced substantially faster trade expansion than the advanced economies in the region, with CAGRs being higher for these economies' exports as well as imports of both goods and services.

■ Trade expansion has been relatively rapid for all of the developing subregions, with the Central Asia subregion being the only one with below-average growth for goods as well as services.

The data in Table 1.2 offer greater detail on trade for several of the region's most significant goods sectors. When one averages out the data for 2020–2022, thus minimizing the short-term impact of the pandemic, it is clear that growth rates since the 2005–2007 period remained positive. It is notable that the sectors with the highest rates of export growth are also those with the highest rates of import growth. That trend may reflect a repositioning along the value chains with more complex goods showing higher rates of growth for exports than imports. For the food sector, raw agricultural products and fuels, where imports have grown faster than exports, the trends may be more greatly affected by supply chains disruptions, trade restrictions, prices volatility, as well as population growth.

Developing Asia's trade in services is also recovering. All subregions suffered contractions in their services trade at the pandemic's onset, and in 2020, Central Asia and the Pacific subregions' services exports shrunk faster than those of Asia's advanced economies. The region's services exports bounced back in 2021, with developing Asia's growth outpacing that of Asia's advanced economies. Apart from travel services, which severely suffered during the pandemic as a result of cross-border and mobility restrictions, services trade exhibited positive growth rates in 2021. Furthermore, East Asia and South Asia continue to increase their shares in global services exports.

Table 1.2: Growth in Asia and Pacific Trade in Selected Goods Sectors, 2005–2022
(3-year average values, $ billion and CAGR)

Goods	Exports			Imports		
	2005–2007 ($)	2020–2022 ($)	CAGR (%)	2005–2007 ($)	2020–2022 ($)	CAGR (%)
Food	110.1	338.7	7.78	105.0	471.3	10.53
Raw agriculture	33.7	61.9	4.14	61.1	119.4	4.57
Fuels	216.0	396.2	4.13	522.1	1,225.9	5.86
Iron and steel	82.9	183.3	5.43	93.7	148.3	3.11
Chemicals	191.3	595.4	7.86	250.6	657.7	6.64
Machinery	1,298.2	3,373.6	6.57	1,079.1	2,597.3	6.03
Textiles	111.8	225.0	4.78	55.7	93.0	3.48
Clothing	176.9	314.2	3.90	29.7	45.6	2.91

CAGR = compound annual growth rate.
Notes: CAGR is calculated on the basis of 15 intervals for goods and 14 for services. Data on services trade are not yet available for 2022. Advanced Asia comprises Australia, Japan, and New Zealand. Developing Asia comprises Central Asia, East Asia, South Asia, Southeast Asia, and the Pacific.
Source: Asian Development Bank calculations using data from the World Trade Organization at https://stats.wto.org/ (accessed 31 January 2024).

Although the data are more aggregated for trade in services than for goods, and thus allow for less detailed analysis, the information in Table 1.3 offers some insights. The region's highest rates of trade growth, both for exports and imports, have been in the wide range of activities that fall under the broad definition of "other commercial services." The strong rate of growth in these services offers a good measure of shifts in the overall economic composition of the region, if not all of its subregions, insofar as many of these services are more capital- and knowledge-intensive than are the more labor-intensive and traditional mainstays of the region's merchandise exports. Revealing comparisons can therefore be made between exports of these commercial services on the one hand and the more established textile and clothing industries on the other. Comparing data from Tables 1.2 and 1.3, one may see that as of 2005–2007, the region exported $1.91 worth of textiles and clothing for every $1 worth of these other commercial services; by 2020–2021, it was exporting $0.98 worth of textiles and clothing for every $1 worth of these other commercial services.

Table 1.3: Growth in Asia and Pacific Trade in Services, 2005–2021
(3-year average values, $ billion and CAGR)

Services	Exports			Imports		
	2005–2007 ($)	2020–2021 ($)	CAGR (%)	2005–2007 ($)	2020–2021 ($)	CAGR (%)
Goods-related	35.3	59.4	3.54	30.1	54.0	3.97
Travel	109.6	150.6	2.14	121.0	256.4	5.14
Transport	140.4	273.3	4.54	140.4	291.7	5.00
Other	150.8	552.0	9.03	173.2	552.8	8.04

CAGR = compound annual growth rate.
Notes: CAGR is calculated on the basis of 14 intervals. Other is other commercial services. Goods-related services include manufacturing services on physical inputs owned by others, and maintenance and repair services not included elsewhere. Other commercial services include construction, insurance and pension services, financial services, charges for the use of intellectual property not included elsewhere, telecommunications, computer, and information services, other business services, and personal, cultural, and recreational services.
Source: Asian Development Bank calculations using data from World Trade Organization. WTO Stats. https://stats.wto.org/ (accessed 31 January 2024).

Overall Direction and Growth of Trade in Environmental Goods and Services

While there is no universally accepted definition of environmental goods and services (EGS), they are typically understood to encompass goods and services utilized to gauge, prevent, restrict, diminish, or rectify environmental harm to water, air, and soil, as well as issues associated with waste, noise, and ecosystems (OECD and Statistical Office of the European Communities 1999). These include cleaner technologies, products, and services aimed at mitigating environmental risks and reducing pollution and resource consumption.[2] For purely analytical purposes, we have used the

---

[2] The WTO Trade and Environmental Sustainability Structure Discussions (TESSD) Working Group on Environmental Goods and Services is exploring opportunities and possible approaches to promoting and facilitating trade in environmental goods and services to meet climate goals, including in the sector of renewable energy.

broad Combined List of Environmental Goods (CLEG) developed by the Organisation for Economic Co-operation and Development (OECD). The CLEG is derived from a combination of the OECD's indicative plurilateral environmental goods and services list, lists of environmental goods submitted by WTO members in such coalitions as "Friends Groups," (WTO 2009) and the Asia-Pacific Economic Cooperation (APEC) list.[3] The resulting combined list consists of 248 products at the six-digit level of the Harmonized System 2007 nomenclature (Sauvage 2014).

The data in Table 1.4 show that the Asia and Pacific region enjoys a substantial environmental goods (EG) trade surplus, with its collective exports to the world being two-thirds larger than its imports in 2022. The data also show a high concentration of trade in this sector, with relatively small numbers of economies accounting for most of the trade and only half a dozen being net exporters. The single largest provider (the People's Republic of China [PRC]) accounted for over half of the region's EG exports in 2022, the next five for nearly one-third, and the next five for over one-tenth. Taken together, those 11 major exporters supplied 98.9% of the region's EG exports in 2022; the remaining 1.1% was shared among 18 other economies. Imports are also concentrated, but not nearly to the same degree; the 11 largest exporters took in 88.1% of the region's EG imports.

Table 1.4: Asia and Pacific Economies' Trade in Environmental Goods, 2022

(exports to and imports from the world, $ million and percentages)

	Exports ($)	Share (%)	Imports ($)	Share (%)	Balance ($)
Net Exporters					
PRC	443,863.8	56.78	127,349.3	27.23	316,514.5
Japan	99,097.0	12.68	48,677.9	10.41	50,419.1
Republic of Korea	60,418.6	7.73	48,461.8	10.36	11,956.8
Malaysia	24,553.3	3.14	18,075.4	3.86	6,477.9
Singapore	35,656.9	4.56	33,870.0	7.24	1,786.9
Cambodia	2,496.2	0.32	2,266.3	0.48	229.9
Net Importers					
Viet Nam	23,238.1	2.97	23,288.3	4.98	−50.2
Fiji	2.9	<0.01	145.5	0.03	−142.6
Sri Lanka	693.5	0.09	894.3	0.19	−200.8
Brunei Darussalam	91.6	0.01	319.0	0.07	−227.4
Maldives	0.1	<0.01	296.7	0.06	−296.7
Tajikistan	4.9	<0.01	313.6	0.07	−308.6
Armenia	112.6	0.01	502.1	0.11	−389.5

continued on next page

---

[3]   The Asia-Pacific Economic Cooperation (APEC) list consists of 54 products, emerged from nominations by member economies of the APEC forum, as part of an effort to attain early voluntary liberalization of trade in particular sectors. See Steenblick (2005).

Table 1.4 *continued*

	Exports ($)	Share (%)	Imports ($)	Share (%)	Balance ($)
Kyrgyz Republic	44.7	0.01	534.0	0.11	−489.3
Myanmar	173.4	0.02	823.9	0.18	−650.5
Nepal	19.0	<0.01	681.9	0.15	−662.9
Georgia	20.5	<0.01	937.8	0.20	−917.3
Mongolia	13.2	<0.01	1,069.9	0.23	−1,056.7
Azerbaijan	51.3	0.01	1,666.3	0.36	−1,614.9
Pakistan	115.6	0.01	2,865.0	0.61	−2,749.4
Uzbekistan	155.9	0.02	2,951.3	0.63	−2,795.3
Hong Kong, China	24,296.5	3.11	27,791.1	5.94	−3,494.6
India	24,735.0	3.16	28,652.6	6.13	−3,917.6
Thailand	24,156.7	3.09	28,270.3	6.04	−4,113.5
Philippines	4,872.0	0.62	9,145.0	1.96	−4,273.0
New Zealand	871.9	0.11	5,310.5	1.14	−4,438.7
Kazakhstan	688.9	0.09	5,189.6	1.11	−4,500.7
Indonesia	7,507.6	0.96	18,627.0	3.98	−11,119.4
Australia	3,827.0	0.49	28,757.3	6.15	−24,930.3
Region Total	**781,778.8**	**100.00**	**467,733.7**	**100.00**	**314,045.2**

PRC = People's Republic of China.
Notes: The table includes goods related to air pollution control, cleaner or more resource-efficient technologies and products, environmentally preferable products based on end use or disposal characteristics, heat and energy management, environmental monitoring, analysis and assessment equipment, natural resources protection, noise and vibration abatement, renewable energy plant, management of solid and hazardous waste and recycling systems, clean up or remediation of soil and water, and wastewater management and potable water treatment. Data are not available, or values are zero, for Kiribati, the Lao People's Democratic Republic, Papua New Guinea, and Samoa. Effective 1 February 2021, ADB placed a temporary hold on sovereign project disbursements and new contracts in Myanmar.
Source: Asian Development Bank calculations using data from World Integrated Trade Solution (WITS) and UNCOMTRADE Database. https://wits.worldbank.org/ (accessed 31 May 2024).

When one turns to intraregional EG trade, as shown in Figure 1.3, the pattern shifts. The intraregional environmental goods trade is an indicator under the environmental cooperation dimension in the regional cooperation and integration index. It is the proportion of intraregional environmental goods trade (exports plus imports) to total intraregional goods trade.[4] East Asia remains the principal player, but its trade in this sector comprised a smaller share of total intraregional trade in 2018–2021 than it had in the preceding periods. Over that same time, other subregions (apart from the Pacific) saw fairly steady growth in their shares. The relative shifting of the proportion of EG trade in total trade from East Asia to Advanced Asia, Southeast Asia, South Asia, and Central Asia from 2006 to 2021 may be attributed to such factors as trade diversion from preferential trade agreements (PTAs) covering environmental goods, diversification, and derisking within global supply chains.

---

[4]   For further details on the index see Asia Regional Integration Center. Highlights. https://aric.adb.org/database/arcii/highlights.

Figure 1.4 shows fairly steady growth in the region's 2007–2022 EG exports. Total exports more than tripled during that period, and the region's share of the global EG market rose from one-fourth to two-fifths. The great majority of that growth was achieved by the East Asia and Southeast Asia regions, whose collective share of the region's exports rose from two-thirds in 2007 to four-fifths in 2022. Except for the Pacific, all the subregions experienced an increase in EG exports during the

Figure 1.3: Asia and Pacific Intraregional Environmental Goods Trade, 2006–2021
(percentage of total intraregional goods trade, 4-year averages)

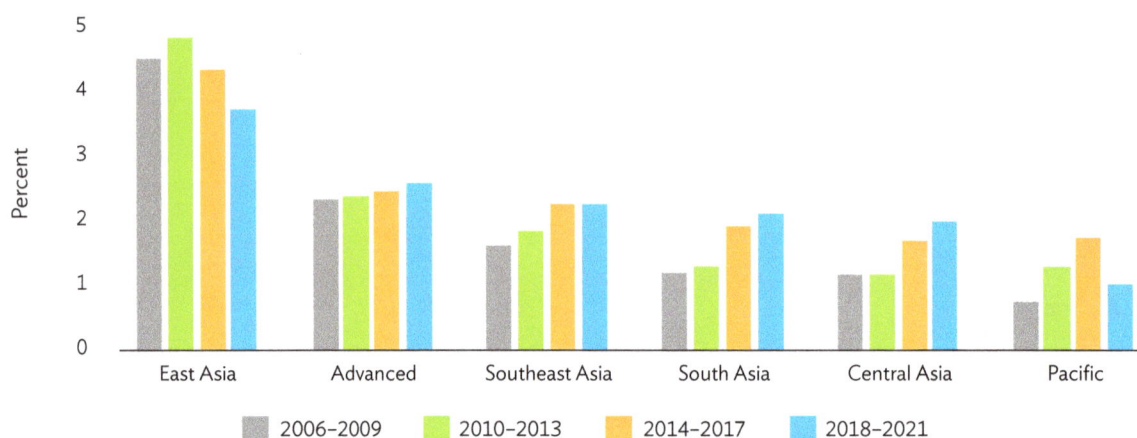

Source: Asian Development Bank. Asia-Pacific Regional Cooperation and Integration Index Database. https://aric.adb.org/database/arcii/indicators.

Figure 1.4: Total Asia and Pacific Exports of Environmental Goods, 2007–2022

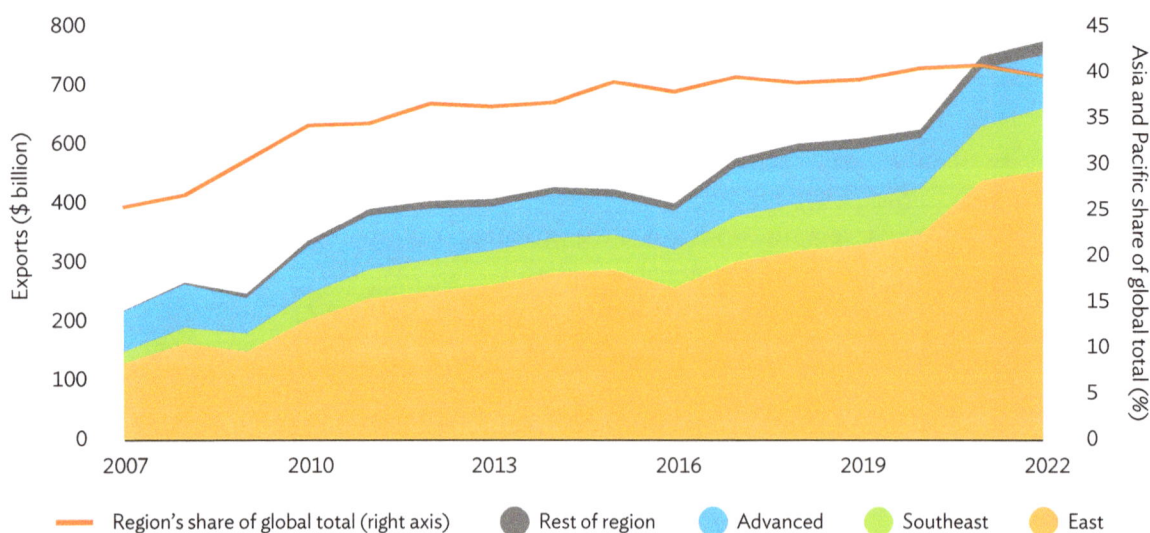

Notes: Rest of Region is Central Asia, South Asia, and Pacific subregions. Advanced Asia comprises Australia, Japan, and New Zealand.
Source: Asian Development Bank calculations using data from World Integrated Trade Solution (WITS) and UNCOMTRADE Database.

COVID-19 pandemic. This could be a result of the adoption of stringent environmental policies and net-zero targets of major emitters of the Asia and Pacific region. Developing Asia's share in global EG exports increased from 18% in 2007 to 35% in 2021, with the share even increasing during the pandemic, albeit with a slight decline in the recovery phase.

Figure 1.5 offers further detail on the types of goods that predominate in the Asia and Pacific EG exports. Renewable energy plant has been the largest contributor to CLEG exports throughout this period, but its export growth has not been very rapid. Most of the rise in the region's EG exports has been in three other subsectors: wastewater management and potable water treatment, cleaner or more resource-efficient technologies, and environmental monitoring, analysis and assessment equipment. Ever since 2020, those three subsectors have collectively accounted for a larger share of the region's EG exports than does renewable energy plant.

Figure 1.5: Asia and Pacific Exports of Environmental Goods by Type, 2007–2022

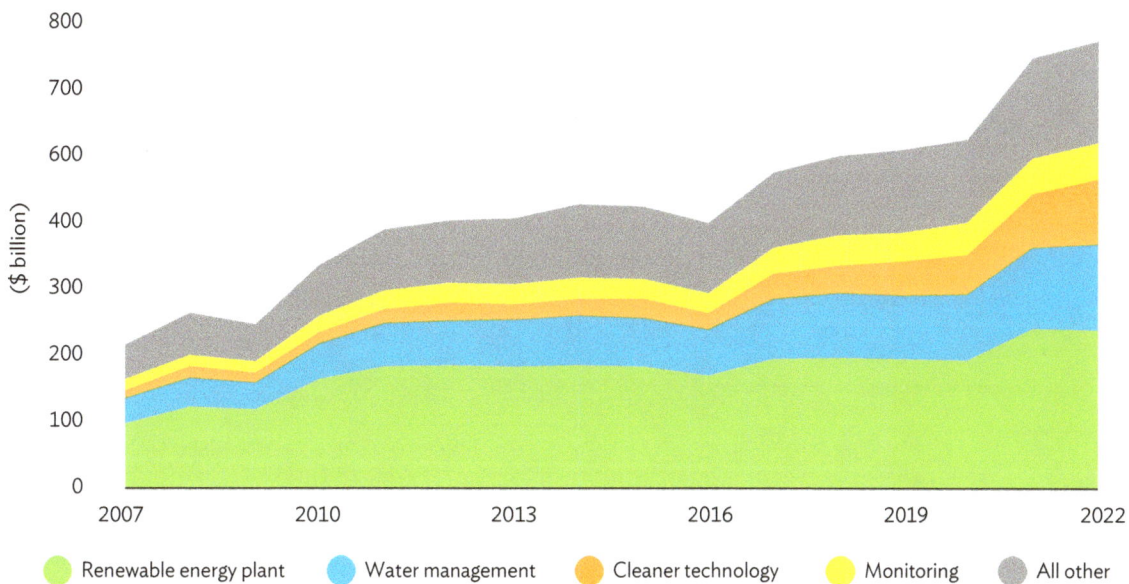

Notes: Monitoring refers to environmental monitoring, analysis, and assessment equipment. Cleaner tech refers to cleaner or more resource-efficient technologies and products. Water management refers to wastewater management and potable water treatment. All other includes air pollution control, environmentally preferable products based on end use or disposal characteristics, heat and energy management, natural resources protection, noise and vibration abatement, management of solid and hazardous waste and recycling systems, and clean up or remediation of soil and water.
Source: Asian Development Bank calculations using data from World Integrated Trade Solution (WITS) and UNCOMTRADE Database.

Turning to imports, Figure 1.6 illustrates a pair of contrasting trends. Total Asia and Pacific EG imports rose over the period of 2007–2022, yet a few downturns punctuated the generally upward pattern. Moreover, the region's share of the global total changed markedly. Whereas it rose from less than one-quarter in 2007 to nearly one-third in 2013, it declined thereafter; by 2022, it was back down to about one-quarter (25.3%). Although East Asia has been importing almost half of the environmental goods into the region, there has been a relative shift toward Southeast Asia, Advanced Asia, Central Asia, South Asia, and the Pacific.

Figure 1.6: Total Asia and Pacific Imports of Environmental Goods, 2007–2022

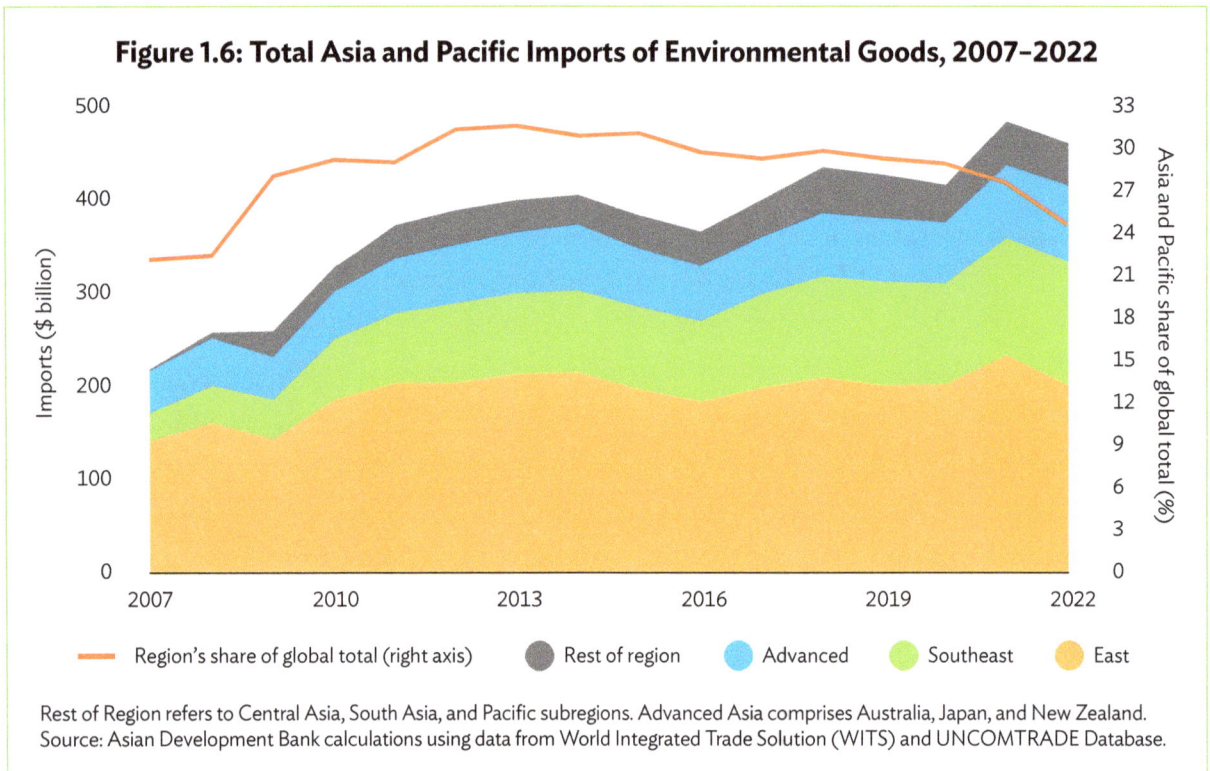

Rest of Region refers to Central Asia, South Asia, and Pacific subregions. Advanced Asia comprises Australia, Japan, and New Zealand.
Source: Asian Development Bank calculations using data from World Integrated Trade Solution (WITS) and UNCOMTRADE Database.

Figure 1.7 likewise shows that renewable energy plant holds a large but declining share, and the same three subsectors that showed the greatest growth in exports do the same for imports. Import growth has nonetheless been slower than export growth, both overall and for individual subsectors. Whereas total EG imports approximately doubled between 2007 and 2022, exports more than tripled over that same period. And while the region's EG exports rose every year from 2017 through 2022, its imports declined in three of those years (including 2022).

Figure 1.7: Asia and Pacific Imports of Environmental Goods by Type, 2007–2022

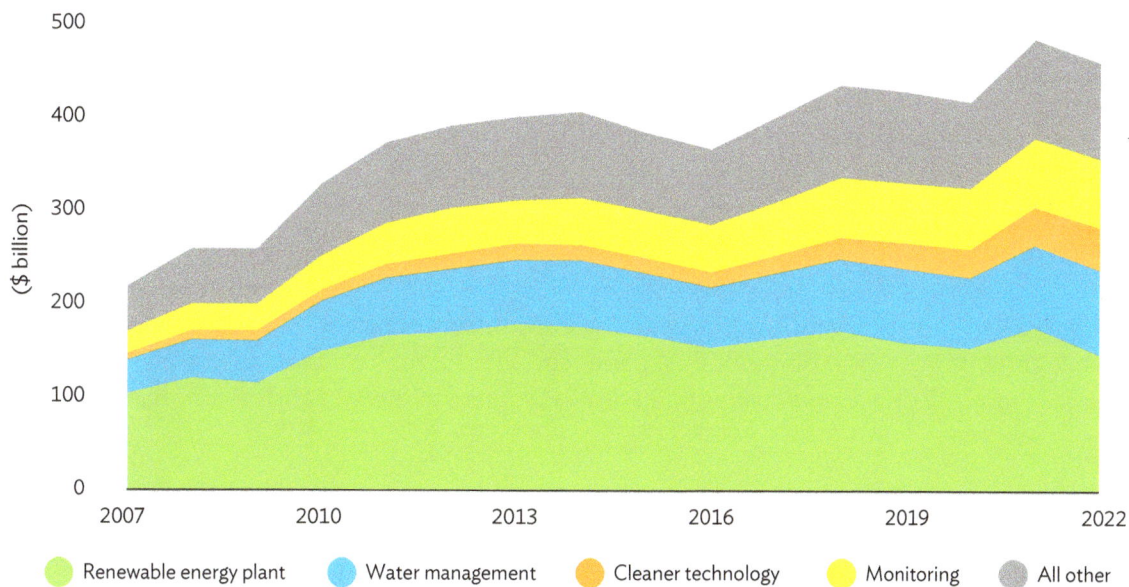

Notes: All other includes air pollution control, environmentally preferable products based on end use or disposal characteristics, heat and energy management, natural resources protection, noise and vibration abatement, management of solid and hazardous waste and recycling systems, and clean up or remediation of soil and water. Monitoring refers to environmental monitoring, analysis, and assessment equipment. Cleaner technology refers to cleaner or more resource efficient technologies and products. Water management refers to wastewater management and potable water treatment. All other includes air pollution control, environmentally preferable products based on end use or disposal characteristics, heat and energy management, natural resources protection, noise and vibration abatement, management of solid and hazardous waste and recycling systems, and clean up or remediation of soil and water.
Source: Asian Development Bank calculations using data from World Integrated Trade Solution (WITS) and UNCOMTRADE Database.

Chapter 2

Recent Trends in Aid for Trade

Overall Direction and Growth of Aid for Trade

The unprecedented COVID-19 pandemic affected global AfT disbursements. Three years since the pandemic's outbreak, however, AfT disbursement trends in Asia and the Pacific are recuperating and are now at the highest level in 2 decades.

After registering double-digit growth from 2002 to 2009, and still rising in 2010–2020, the growth in global AfT disbursements slowed to less than 1% in 2020. As may be seen from the data in Figure 2.1, the Asia and Pacific region and Africa have rather consistently been the largest recipients of this aid. While other regions have sometimes experienced short-term increases, as was the case for the Middle East in 2005–2007 and Europe in 2011–2016, the combined Asian/African share is typically

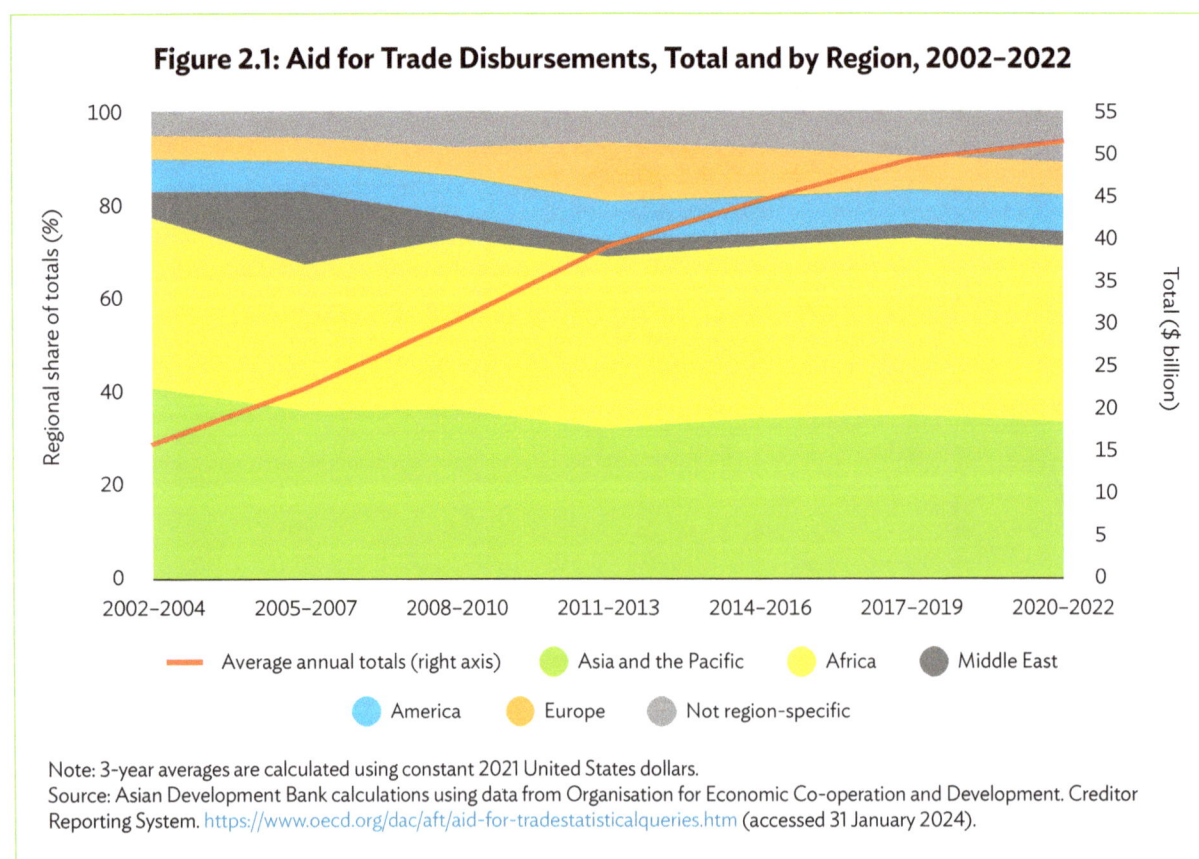

Figure 2.1: Aid for Trade Disbursements, Total and by Region, 2002–2022

Note: 3-year averages are calculated using constant 2021 United States dollars.
Source: Asian Development Bank calculations using data from Organisation for Economic Co-operation and Development. Creditor Reporting System. https://www.oecd.org/dac/aft/aid-for-tradestatisticalqueries.htm (accessed 31 January 2024).

in the range of two-thirds to three-quarters of the total. As of 2020–2022, it was 71.1%; the Asia and Pacific share was 33.6%, down from 35.0% in 2017–2019. That most recent decline in the Asia and Pacific share of AfT disbursements coincided with the pandemic years. In 2020, AfT disbursements to the Pacific subregion and South Asia most significantly contracted, while disbursements increased significantly in Central Asia and especially East Asia.

Total official development assistance (ODA) increased across all developing Asia subregions in 2020, driven mostly by social infrastructure and services. As a result, AfT as a share of ODA declined. That trend reversed in 2021, when ODA flows and AfT disbursements increased in the Pacific and South Asia subregions. A more pronounced rebound was observed in 2022, when the share of AfT in ODA increased across all subregions due to faster growth of AfT flows compared to ODA. Compared to 2021, East Asia increased its share of AfT in ODA by about 14 percentage points in 2022, followed by South Asia (8.6 percentage points), Southeast Asia (8 percentage points), and the Pacific subregion (5 percentage points). Central Asia, where the share of AfT in ODA increased by 4 percentage points in 2021, further increased its share by 1.5 percentage points in 2022. As shown in Figure 2.2, the Asia and Pacific donor economies continue to be the largest source of AfT funds. These donors had provided just under half the funds in 2021, and in 2022, their contributions of $10.9 billion amounted to 56.1% of the total. The Asian Development Bank (ADB) and other multilateral donors provided another $5.4 billion in 2022 (27.9% of the total), while the remaining $3.1 billion (16.1%) came from all other donors.

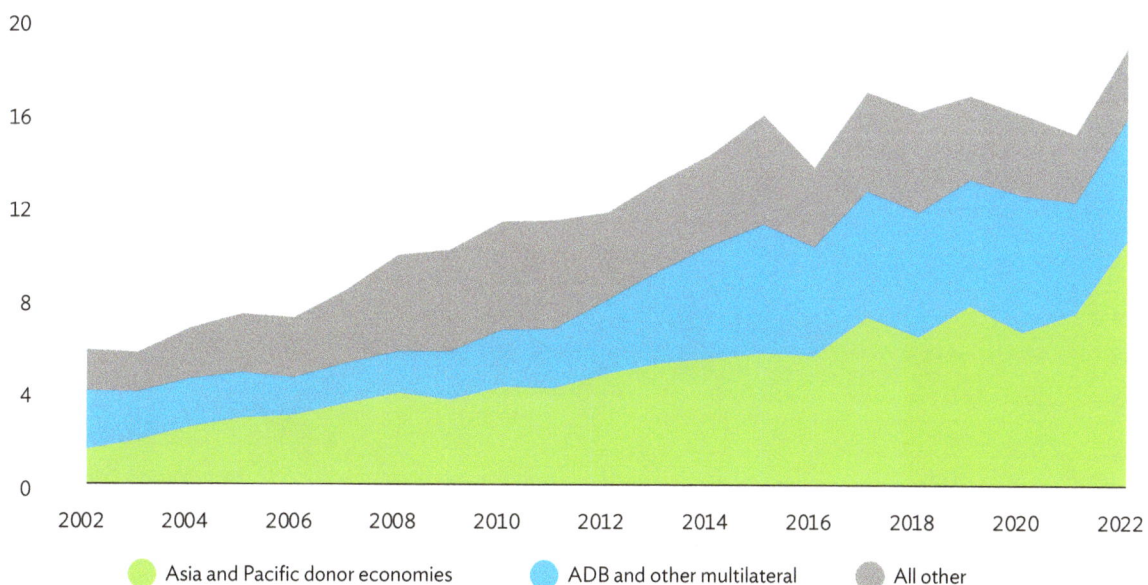

Figure 2.2: Aid for Trade Disbursements to Developing Asia by Type of Donors, 2002–2022
($ billion)

Notes: Other multilaterals include European Union institutions, the Islamic Development Bank, United Nations organizations, and the World Bank Group. Data is in constant 2021 United States dollars.
Source: Asian Development Bank calculations using data from the Organisation for Economic Co-operation and Development. Creditor Reporting System. https://stats.oecd.org/Index.aspx?DataSetCode=crs1# (accessed 28 February 2024).

South Asia continues to receive the greatest share of AfT flows among Asian subregions, as made plain by the data in Figure 2.3. This is a long-term trend, with that region receiving the largest share of AfT disbursements every year, and at least half in all years since 2017; in 2022 the South Asia share was 55.7%. Southeast Asia remains the second-highest recipient of AfT flows, typically receiving between one-fourth and one-third of the total; in 2022, its share was 28.0%. Smaller shares in 2022 went to Central Asia (9.8%), the Pacific (3.4%), and East Asia (3.1%). Taking the longer view, the largest relative decline over time has been for East Asia, where only two economies— Mongolia and the People's Republic of China—are reported to receive aid for trade disbursements. East Asia typically received 14%–15% of the total at the start of the century, it has since declined in both absolute and relative terms. Nine of the top 10 recipients of AfT flows were located in South Asia and Southeast Asia, while seven of the bottom 10 were in the Pacific subregion. These rankings change, however, when disbursements are considered relative to the vastly different sizes of these economies. When viewed on a per capita basis, or as a percentage of gross domestic product (GDP), the Pacific countries dominate the top 10. As may be appreciated from the data in Figure 2.4, AfT flows relative to GDP are vastly higher in the Pacific than in any other subregion. The relative importance of this source in relation to total aid also varies by region. Aid for Trade represented more than half of total ODA disbursements received by India. More than 40% of total ODA was also accounted to AfT among three economies in Southeast Asia (Viet Nam, Thailand, and the Philippines), three economies in Central Asia (Armenia, Uzbekistan, and Tajikistan), Bangladesh in South Asia, and Palau in the Pacific subregion.

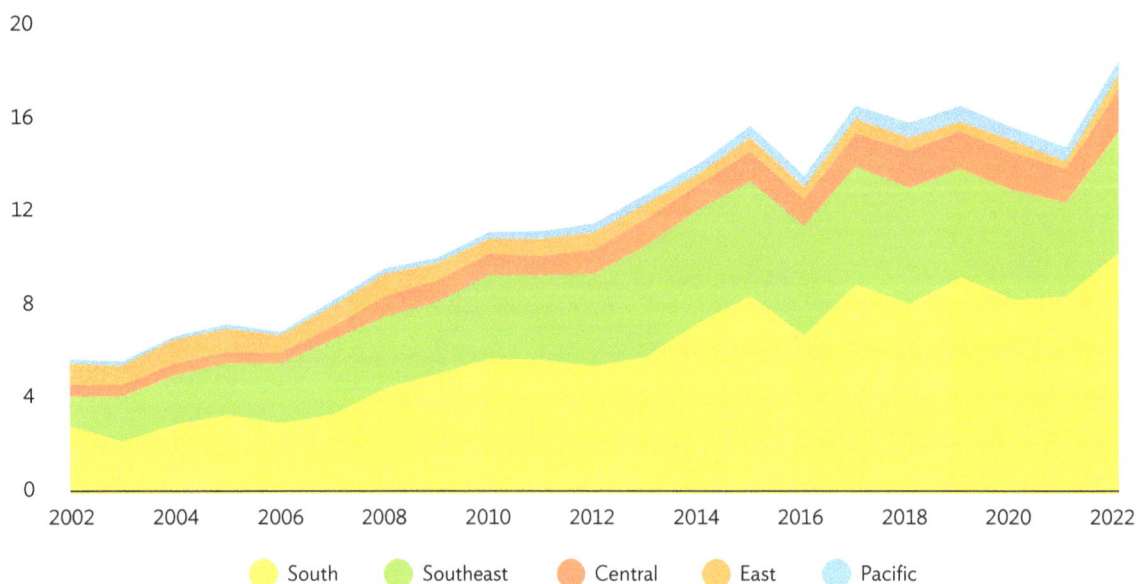

Figure 2.3: Aid for Trade Flows to Developing Asia, 2002–2022
($ billion)

Note: Data is in constant 2021 United States dollars.
Source: Asian Development Bank calculations using data from Organisation for Economic Co-operation and Development. Creditor Reporting System. https://www.oecd.org/dac/aft/aid-for-tradestatisticalqueries.htm (accessed 31 January 2024).

Figure 2.4: Aid for Trade Flows as a Share of GDP, 2002–2022
(%)

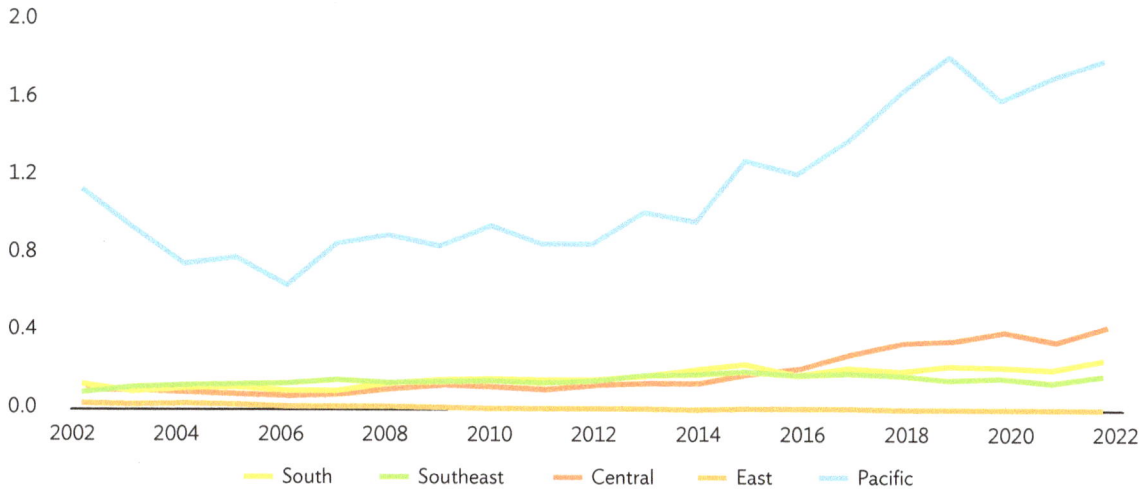

GDP = gross domestic product.
Note: GDP calculated using constant 2021 United States dollars.
Sources: Asian Development Bank (ADB) calculations using data from Organisation for Economic Co-operation and Development. Creditor Reporting System. https://www.oecd.org/dac/aft/aid-for-tradestatisticalqueries.htm (accessed 31 January 2024). For the population and GDP of Niue and the Cook Islands: ADB. Key Indicators for Asia and the Pacific 2023. https://www.adb.org/publications/keyindicators-asia-and-pacific-2023 (accessed 31 January 2024).

Aid for Trade and the Least Developed Countries

The least-developed countries (LDCs) constitute a special group among the developing countries, being designated by the United Nations on the basis of objective criteria and qualifying for special treatment under (among others) rules of the World Trade Organization (WTO). Asia is home to a small and decreasing share of LDCs; several have already graduated from this status, and Afghanistan is the only remaining LDC in the region that is not at some stage of consideration for its future graduation.[5] That is both an achievement and a challenge, as it signifies recognition of a country's development while also removing some of the instruments that helped to achieve this result. With so many Asia and Pacific countries facing the prospect of future graduation, it is important to note the additional challenges posed by such a graduation.

The data in Table 2.1 not only show the relatively high importance of AfT among the LDCs, but also show how this varies among LDCs by other observable criteria. Eight of the 10 remaining LDCs in the region fall into either of two very different categories that face development challenges. The United Nations Conference on Trade and Development lists 32 countries as landlocked developing countries (LLDCs),[6] three of which are in the Asia and Pacific region.

---

[5] For past and present LDC designations, as well as the graduations that are at issue, see UNCTAD. https://unctad.org/topic/least-developed-countries/list. ADB placed its regular assistance to Afghanistan on hold effective 15 August 2021.
[6] See UNCTAD. List of Landlocked Developing Countries. https://unctad.org/topic/landlocked-developing-countries/list-of-LLDCs.

Table 2.1: Aid for Trade to Least Developed Countries in the Asia and Pacific Region, 2002–2022

	Aid for Trade Total ($ million)				Aid for Trade as Share of GDP				Aid for Trade per Capita ($)			
	2002 ($)	2012 ($)	2022 ($)	Change, 2002–2022	2002 (%)	2012 (%)	2022 (%)	Change, 2002–2022	2002 ($)	2012 ($)	2022 ($)	Change, 2002–2022
Small Island Developing					*6.0*	*6.0*	*13.0*	*+7.0*	*139.66*	*191.50*	*452.54*	*$312.88*
Kiribati‡	9.2	27.2	35.1	+$25.9	7.7	10.7	16.4	+8.7	99.42	243.25	267.19	+$167.77
Solomon Islands†	6.0	46.2	85.4	+$79.4	0.7	3.2	5.7	+5.0	13.42	81.34	117.96	+$104.54
Timor-Leste‡	34.3	58.2	64.4	+$30.1	2.8	3.0	2.2	-0.6	37.66	51.19	48.00	+$10.34
Tuvalu‡	3.9	4.2	15.6	+$11.7	12.6	7.2	27.8	+15.2	408.15	390.20	1,377.00	+$968.85
Landlocked Developing					*1.3*	*3.9*	*2.1*	*+0.8*	*15.86*	*49.12*	*37.94*	*$22.08*
Afghanistan	42.7	1,653.8	365.1	+$322.4	0.7	10.9	3.1	+2.4	2.03	54.28	8.88	+$6.85
Bhutan*	21.6	78.2	74.2	+$52.6	1.5	2.7	2.1	+0.6	34.85	108.45	94.82	+$59.97
Lao PDR**	116.0	155.1	235.1	+$119.1	2.2	1.1	1.8	-0.4	20.70	23.82	31.22	+$10.52
Nepal**	148.7	271.7	513.8	+$365.1	0.6	0.7	1.4	+0.8	5.87	9.94	16.82	+$10.95
Other Asia and Pacific LDCs					*0.5*	*0.7*	*1.3*	*+0.8*	*3.37*	*7.90*	*23.84*	*$20.47*
Bangladesh**	416.7	869.9	3,551.7	+$3,135.0	0.3	0.4	0.8	+0.5	3.11	5.72	20.75	+$17.64
Cambodia‡	86.4	254.4	725.2	+$638.8	1.1	1.5	2.6	+1.5	6.88	17.20	43.25	+$36.37
Myanmar‡	5.5	38.5	407.2	+$401.7	<0.1	0.1	0.6	+0.6	0.12	0.77	7.52	+$7.40

GDP = gross domestic product, Lao PDR = Lao People's Democratic Republic, LDC = least developed country.
*   Graduated from LDC status at the end of 2023.
**   Scheduled to graduate in 2026.
†   Scheduled to graduate in 2027.
‡   Candidates for graduation, with deliberations over this change in status at various stages for each country.
Notes: Numbers shown in **Bold Italics** are unweighted averages for subgroups. Most recent GDP shares for Afghanistan and Bhutan are for 2021 rather than 2022. ADB placed its regular assistance to Afghanistan on hold effective 15 August 2021.
Source: Asian Development Bank calculations using data from the Organisation for Economic Co-operation and Development. Creditor Reporting System. https://stats.oecd.org/Index.aspx?DataSetCode=crs1# (accessed 31 January 2024).

Moreover, the region includes four LDCs that are among the 39 economies that the United Nations lists as small island developing states (SIDS).[7] It is precisely those last four countries for which AfT has the highest relative significance. This is most notably the case for Tuvalu: While the $15.6 million in AfT provided to this island state in 2022 was less than 0.5% of the value provided to Bangladesh that year, it amounted to $1,377 per capita and more than one-quarter of the GDP. Or to compare the averages for the four SIDS/LDCs against those of the three regional LDCs that are neither SIDS nor LLDCs, AfT was 19 times larger on a per capita basis and accounted for 10 times the level of the GDP.

---

[7]   See United Nations. List of SIDS. https://www.un.org/ohrlls/content/list-sids.

The LDCs have not been able to achieve the Sustainable Development Goal (SDG) target to double shares of global exports by 2020. The Doha Programme of Action calls for a considerable increase in AfT resources, as well as a greater focus on digital trade. However, there have been consistent shortfalls in AfT disbursements to the LDCs. That gap for LDCs remained at $5.3 billion in 2021, leaving disbursements 28% short of commitments (UNCTAD 2023).

The Enhanced Integrated Framework (EIF) has been the only global AfT program dedicated to addressing the trade capacity needs of LDCs, and the only dedicated AfT program specifically included in the SDGs. Phase 2 of the EIF ended in 2022, however, and the program is currently operating on an interim basis. Deliberations on a new program are ongoing.

LDCs participating in the EIF program have undertaken a periodic assessment of trade potential opportunities and challenges through a diagnostic trade integration study (DTIS) or its update. These studies provide a platform for the integration of priority issues into government policies and donor programming through the identification of an action matrix. Over time, especially for each DTIS developed after 2016, environmental concerns have become more integrated. There nonetheless remains a need for a coherent conceptual framework to integrate climate change adaptation and mitigation objectives. While the Climate Change Development Reports (or Assessing Low Carbon Transition initiative) that the World Bank launched with the World Trade Organization and the World Economic Forum provides new insights to address this limitation, these are not substitutes for a DTIS or similar, which includes recommendations on institutional capabilities and trade governance structures. AfT assistance should also help address LDC graduation challenges (Box 2.1).

Box 2.1: Leveraging Aid for Trade for Smooth Graduation of Least Developed Countries

There are currently 10 least developed countries (LDCs) as defined by the United Nations, in Asia and the Pacific. Four of them are in Southeast Asia (Cambodia, the Lao People's Democratic Republic [Lao PDR], Myanmar, and Timor-Leste), three in South Asia (Afghanistan, Bangladesh, and Nepal), and three in the Pacific subregion (Kiribati, Solomon Islands, and Tuvalu). Four Asia and Pacific countries have already transitioned out of LDC status: Maldives (2011), Samoa (2014), Vanuatu (2020), and most recently Bhutan (December 2023).

Graduation is not just a symbolic status change, but official recognition that a country has accomplished significant economic and social development goals. It also means the loss of benefits such as duty-free quota-free (DFQF) treatment and favorable rules of origin for exports to preference-granting countries, as well as reduced international concessional support. Without careful planning and support to offset these losses, graduated economies could face new challenges that may hamper their development (Crivelli, Inama, and Pascua 2023).

Aid for Trade (AfT) with its focus on enhancing trade capacity, regulations, and infrastructure, can offer vital support during this critical transition. **How can AfT be effectively and strategically utilized to support smooth graduations for LDCs?** Below are suggested recommendations with specific examples:

continued on next page

Box 2.1 *continued*

1. Fostering Trade Expansion and Diversification through Trade Agreements

Most Asian LDCs have benefited from increasing export flows and a trend toward diversification over the years. However, these gains are under threat with the upcoming loss of DFQF market access and the continuous unfolding of new trade agreements in the region. AfT can be used to provide technical assistance and policy advice to graduating LDCs on how to negotiate trade agreements with regional or non-regional partners to maintain and enhance market access and address nontariff measures (Crivelli, Inama, and Pascua 2023). Assistance should also be provided to support domestic reforms and regulatory changes to facilitate compliance with international commitments . For example, AfT could fund a gap analysis and target assistance to support Association of Southeast Asian Nations (ASEAN) LDCs in adopting a negative-list approach to services liberalization.

2. Strengthening Regulatory Frameworks

Enhancing capacity in customs and trade regulations would help expedite trade processes and overcome graduation challenges. Technical assistance through AfT could help ASEAN LDCs, for example, streamline and digitize customs procedures to align with the standards of their group. This would not only reduce export and import processing times but also attract more foreign investment by simplifying the business environment.

3. Investing in Trade Infrastructure, Logistical, and Transportation Networks

In the Lao PDR, an AfT initiative could enhance the efficiency of the East-West Economic Corridor that connects several Southeast Asian countries. By upgrading road and rail links, and streamlining border crossings, the Lao PDR can facilitate easier access to larger markets like Thailand and Viet Nam, reducing trade costs and boosting exports.

4. Harnessing Digitalization for Wider Cross-Border Market Opportunities

Cross-border digital services offer significant potential for economic growth (ADB 2022a). AfT could support graduating LDCs in assessing the benefits of digital economy agreements and free trade agreements with e-commerce and digital trade provisions, and raise capacities for the design and negotiations of such agreements. AfT should also help address affordability, limited digital skills, and the absence of digital regulatory frameworks to deal with such issues as cybercrime and data protection. It can support structural reforms to align domestic regulations with international standards, ensuring a secure and inclusive digital transformation.

5. Investing in Technologies that Support High-Value Added

Projects could focus on boosting the textile industry's move up the value chain by investing in technology that supports high-value garment manufacturing. Additionally, supporting the growth of the agri-food sector can diversify exports and reduce dependence on textiles.

6. Building Human Capital through Education and Training Tailored to Emerging Sectors

AfT could fund studies to identify emerging sectors and develop training programs to ensure a sufficient level and quality of human capital to sustain strategic development plans. In the case of information technology and services, for example, partnerships with tech companies and educational institutions could help develop a workforce skilled in such high-demand areas as software development and digital marketing.

7. Promoting Sustainable Practices

AfT should encourage the integration of sustainable and environmentally friendly methods in key industries. In Solomon Islands, for example, AfT could support the establishment of a green certification scheme for fish exports. This would not only preserve the marine biodiversity but also enhance the marketability of exports in environmentally conscious markets.

Source: Authors.

Investments in Micro, Small, and Medium-Sized Enterprises

It is often noted that micro, small, and medium-sized enterprises (MSMEs) constitute both the vast majority of firms in most parts of the world and a majority of the workforce. Among the main challenges they face are limited access to finance, being subject to more stringent terms from financial institutions. Moreover, they must also deal with regulatory barriers, logistical difficulties, and lack of market access, all of which make it harder for MSMEs to achieve the economies of scale that allow them to match the capacities of larger firms in complying with international standards, conducting market research, and funding an advertising campaign. They also have lower financial resources for attending international trade fairs or business expos needed to improve access to foreign markets. Not only do MSMEs lack the financial capacity to invest in advanced logistical systems, but they also lack the negotiating power due to their smaller size when negotiating agreements with third-party logistics providers. Failure to achieve economies of scale also reduces access to resources and skills and thus constrains productivity. It is quite telling that MSMEs are overrepresented in sectors with lower average labor productivity.

These are problems that ADB and other international institutions now address, starting with the detailed identification of barriers. ADB (2023c) catalogs many burdensome procedures in customs and other regulatory fields that can be quite costly for MSMEs, made all the more difficult by the diversity of procedures in multiple markets. The International Trade Centre's *SME Competitiveness Outlook 2023* catalogs the usual reasons why MSMEs face higher barriers in international trade but also notes their high fragility in times of greater uncertainty, just as WTO (2016) compiles the many trade-related constraints that MSMEs must overcome.

At a more active level, ADB and its partners can help overcome the barriers that MSMEs face in access to credit and other constraints. To cite just a few examples from the numerous projects that have been funded in recent years:

- ADB invested in a 2-year gender bond of around $7.5 million issued by the Joint Stock Company Microfinance Organization Crystal in Georgia to improve financial outcomes for MSMEs owned and operated by women who are disproportionately affected by barriers to participation.[8]

- ADB loaned $103 million to Ping An International Financial Leasing Co. Ltd. to accelerate the energy efficiency improvements in MSMEs.[9] Another investment of $47.4 million to the Bank of Huzhou will scale up energy efficiencies in MSMEs. This program retains a gender component to address the gap in investment in female-led MSMEs.

- An ADB program in Uzbekistan loaned $100 million to improve the operating environment of MSMEs and help them tackle climate change and build long-run disaster resilience.[10]

---

[8] Full details of the program are available here - 56134-001: Crystal Gender Bond Project | Asian Development Bank (adb.org).
[9] Full details of the program are available here - 56099-001: Ping An Leasing Micro, Small, and Medium-Sized Enterprises Energy Efficiency Improvement Project | Asian Development Bank (adb.org).
[10] Full details of the program are available here - 42007-021: Small and Medium-Sized Enterprises Development Program (Subprogram 2) | Asian Development Bank (adb.org).

- Another $750,000 loan in Sri Lanka will increase MSME competitiveness while also improving both their mitigation and adaptation outcomes to climate change.[11]

- ADB loaned $100 million to a transport company in India (Shriram Transport Finance Company) to facilitate the access of MSMEs to the transport and logistics sector.[12] This program also has a particular focus on the agriculture sector, where vulnerabilities of MSMEs' access to logistics often leads to high levels of waste and financial losses.

- A program jointly administered by Australia and ADB will upgrade physical infrastructure in Solomon Islands to improve the prospects of domestic industry, including MSMEs often located in rural regions, while enhancing the country's adaptation and mitigation approaches to climate change.[13]

- An ADB financing facility of $450 million to the PRC aims to improve market access for MSMEs by improving the provision of market information for local trades, enhancing their ability to access common e-platforms, and upgrading trade facilitation measures for cross-border e-commerce.[14] This program also aims to expand public goods which are required to enhance climate change mitigation and adaptation.

- An Australian program weaves together market access for women-run MSMEs in the Pacific with helping said MSMEs navigate the risk caused by climate change and assisting in the provision of infrastructure aimed at both mitigation and adaptation. The program operates under the aegis of the Australia Pacific Climate Partnership.[15]

Aid for Trade Disbursements by Purpose

Broken down by broad category, the data in Figure 2.5 show that economic infrastructure remains the largest category in cumulative AfT disbursements. Most aid for trade is directed to economic infrastructure, while flows targeting trade policies and regulations remain limited. Looking at more specific levels of economic activity, Figure 2.6 shows that the top sectors supported by AfT are unchanged, notwithstanding the pandemic. Transport and storage continue to receive close to half of AfT disbursements in the region. About half of the remainder went to energy, followed by agriculture, banking, and industry. These top five sectors comprised more than 90% of total AfT disbursements in 2020–2022.

---

[11] Full details of the program are available here - 56093-001: Supporting the Development of Economic Zones and Small and Medium-Sized Enterprise Dynamism to Boost Competitiveness and Jobs | Asian Development Bank (adb.org).

[12] Full details of the program are available here - Shriram Transport Finance Supporting Access to Finance for Small Commercial Vehicle Operators Project: Report and Recommendation of the President | Asian Development Bank (adb.org).

[13] Full details of the program are available here - 46499-002: Sustainable Transport Infrastructure Improvement Program | Asian Development Bank (adb.org).

[14] Full details of the program are available here - 50050-005: Guangxi Regional Cooperation and Integration Promotion Investment Program - Tranche 3 | Asian Development Bank (adb.org).

[15] Further details of the program are available at Australian Government, Department of Foreign Affairs and Trade. Empowering Women's Economic Development in Solomon Islands.

Figure 2.5: Distribution of Aid for Trade Inflows to Asia and the Pacific by Category
(3-year averages)

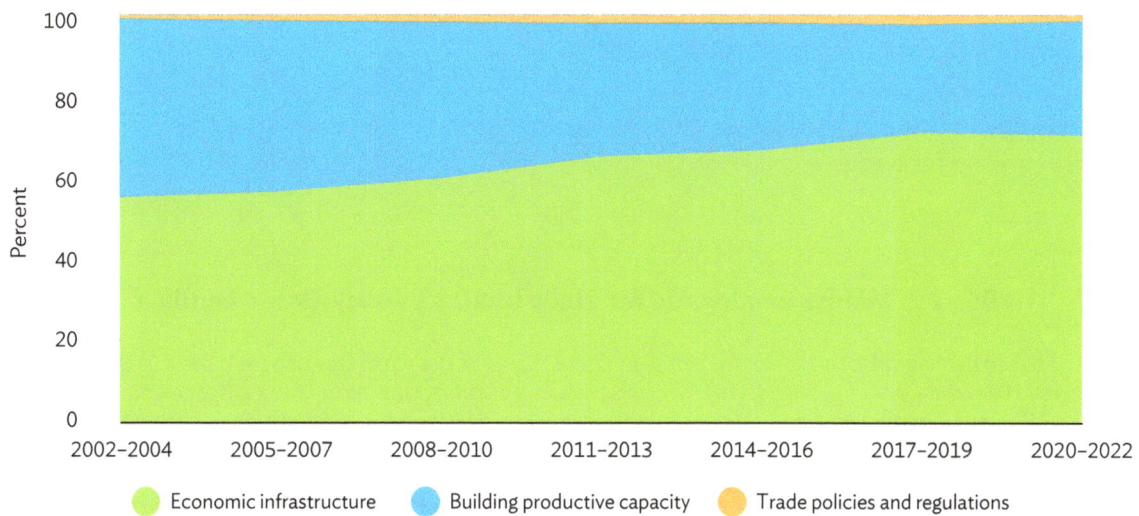

Note: Total aid for trade is the sum of aid for infrastructure, aid for building productive capacity and trade policy and regulations, and trade-related adjustment.
Source: Asian Development Bank calculations using data from Organisation for Economic Co-operation and Development. Creditor Reporting System. https://www.oecd.org/dac/aft/aid-for-tradestatisticalqueries.htm (accessed 31 January 2024).

Figure 2.6: Distribution of Aid for Trade Inflows to Asia and the Pacific by Sector

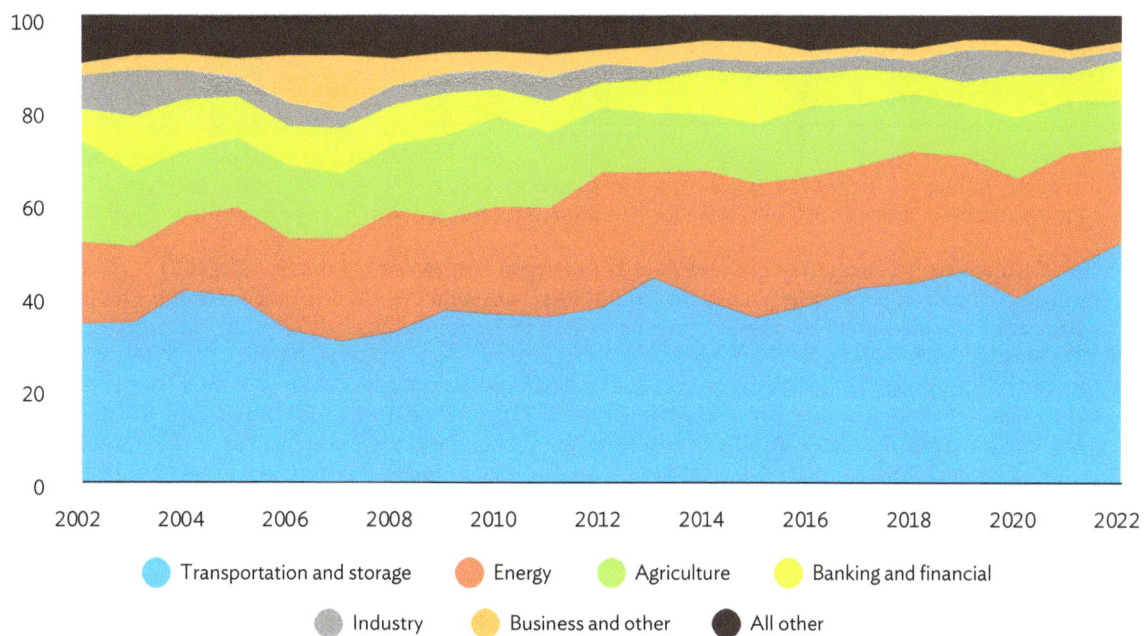

Source: Asian Development Bank calculations using data from the Organisation for Economic Co-operation and Development. Creditor Reporting System. https://www.oecd.org/dac/aft/aid-for-tradestatisticalqueries.htm (accessed 31 January 2024).

AfT flows targeting the trade policies and regulations category remain mostly directed to individual countries. Country-specific disbursements accounted for more than 90% of total AfT flows on trade-related adjustment, multilateral trade negotiations, as well as trade policy and administrative management in 2020–2022. More than 80% of allocations for trade education/training and trade facilitation are also country-specific disbursements.

As summarized in Box 2.2, ADB's policy-based lending projects help many Asia and Pacific countries to mainstream aid for trade.

Box 2.2: Mainstreaming Aid for Trade in ADB's Policy-Based Lending

Policy-based lending (PBL) is the instrument of budget support of the Asian Development Bank (ADB), disbursed in exchange for implementation of critical reforms by the borrowing county's government. Several PBL operations mainstreamed trade into their program designs, for both trade liberalization and trade facilitation. As illustrated below, ADB's Trade and Competitiveness Program for Pakistan successfully mainstreamed trade liberalization into its program design, whereas a series of budget support has been provided to other South Asian economies primarily for implantation of the Trade Facilitation Agreement of the World Trade Organization (WTO). Trade-related PBL is also picking up in the Association of Southeast Asian Nations member states.

Trade and Competitiveness Program for Pakistan. Pakistan faced prolonged balance-of-payments difficulties, and it was critical to mitigate the anti-export bias built into its tariff and tax structures. In partnership with the International Monetary Fund, ADB provided PBL to support Pakistan's reform to cut tariffs and broader trade-related taxes through two subprograms implemented in 2019–2020. Under the program, the government rationalized and lowered the applied tariffs on selected tariff lines. It also reduced (or abolished) regular duties on several raw materials and intermediate inputs, corporate tax, and electricity surcharge on industries. These were supplemented by other measures to mainstream trade into broader reforms, such as a single window for trade facilitation.

Trade and Competitiveness Program for Cambodia. In 2023, a trade and competitiveness program was also approved for Cambodia to enhance the investment and business environment, support the development and diversification of micro, small, and medium-sized enterprises, and help Cambodia improve the implementation of regional trade agreements and strengthen trade facilitation. With $50 million PBL under subprogram 1, the government has enacted a new investment law to codify legal protections for investors, set up the National Committee on Trade Facilitation, and approved the National Road Map on Trade Facilitation.

Trade Facilitation Programs under South Asia Subregional Economic Cooperation (SASEC). ADB has long been providing PBL for trade facilitation in South Asia. Further to the SASEC Trade Facilitation Program for Bangladesh, Bhutan, and Nepal implemented in 2013–2014, the Customs Reforms and Modernization for Trade Facilitation Program for Nepal was approved in 2017 to help the country fulfill its commitment under the WTO's Trade Facilitation Agreement and related international standards on customs. The Customs and Logistics Reform Program, originally approved in 2023, is expanding the government's efforts for trade facilitation to the logistics sector. Another budget support to implement the Trade Facilitation Agreement was approved for Bangladesh as part of the Integrated Trade Facilitation Sector Development Program in 2022.

Competitiveness, Industrial Modernization, and Trade Acceleration Program for Indonesia.
Originally approved in 2021, ADB's PBL supports the government's reforms aimed at improving the business environment and investment climate for manufacturing industries. It also supports trade facilitation and enhancement of logistic services.

Sources: ADB (2017) and ADB (2022b, 2022c, and 2022d).

Navigating Climate Policy Dynamics for Sustainable Trade Competitiveness

Chapter 3

The Twin Problems of Climate Change and Competitiveness

The second part of this report is founded on the premise that a shift toward a low-carbon economy could be bolstered by ambitious, credible, and timely climate policies. Measures to alleviate uncertainty in low-carbon investments are imperative, and the advancement and acceptance of environmental technologies may hinge on precisely targeted and sufficiently funded investments in energy and infrastructure. A robust, quality infrastructure system can also play a vital role in guaranteeing the provision of high-quality environmental goods and services.[16] Policies should also be designed so as to be politically sustainable.

The need to mitigate the effects of climate change is often seen through the lens of trade, and vice versa, as these intersectional issues can reinforce or undermine one another. As highlighted in the *Asian Economic Integration Report 2023*, trade can be a part of the solution when globalization allows the production of energy-intensive goods in locations with the best low-carbon energy potentials, enables new technologies, and synergizes multinational efforts to reduce carbon emissions. Conversely, it can exacerbate climate change by encouraging production and/or shifting production to locations with high emissions intensity, therefore raising carbon emissions.

Global negotiations over how to respond to climate change continue to underline the extent to which costs—both of action and inaction—are distributed asymmetrically. The Asia and Pacific region is a net exporter of carbon emissions, and economies are at risk from more than one direction at a time: Some of them are especially susceptible to damage from climate change; they generally have lower carbon competitiveness than their advanced economy peers in the United States (US) and the European Union, as they continue to attract the largest share of foreign direct investment (FDI) in carbon-intensive industries, which makes it more costly to come into compliance; and they may face heightened barriers in accessing the markets of those partners that choose to erect border barriers to high-carbon goods.

One major point made throughout this report is that the economically most advanced Asian economies are better positioned to put their economies on a low-carbon development path, and to reduce risks to competitiveness, than are their poorer neighbors. They tend to have the most ambitious net-zero targets and nationally determined contributions (NDCs) and have already implemented national climate policies. Some have a carbon price, while others are still considering it. Decarbonization will be a more substantial challenge for countries in Central Asia, where most countries have fewer climate policies, emission targets are less ambitious, and fossil fuel subsidies are high.

---

[16] Quality infrastructure refers to the comprehensive system of public and private institutions, policies, and practices necessary to ensure the quality, safety, and efficiency of products, services, and processes.

Although developing Asian economies overtook the developed economies shortly after the turn of the century as contributors to carbon dioxide (CO_2) emissions, the Asia and Pacific region has achieved significant declines in carbon intensity (i.e., the amount of CO_2 emitted per unit of economic value created). That progress can be seen in Figure 3.1, which shows the values of carbon intensity in 2015 constant US dollars for most of the region. The Asia and Pacific region's carbon intensity declined from 0.77 in 2012 to 0.59 in 2022; while intensity did rise for 13 economies, usually by relatively small amounts, it declined in 29 others. Most of the larger economies in the region were among those for which carbon intensity declined; these included Australia, the People's Republic of China, India, Japan, the Republic of Korea, and New Zealand.

The two countries where emissions rose the most are Cambodia and the Lao People's Democratic Republic (Lao PDR), both of which are LDCs. This observation reiterates the need (as already discussed in Part 1) to leverage Aid for Trade (AfT) to support energy transition in these economies. ADB's Climate Adaptation Investment Planning supports developing member countries (DMCs) in translating their national adaptation priorities for key sectors into adaptation investment plans that will identify a suite of priority investments needed to achieve the country's adaptation goals (ADB 2023e).

Several factors can explain the general trend toward decarbonization, including structural change toward less energy- and emissions-intensive sectors, the deployment of less carbon-intensive energy sources, and more efficient energy use. Most Asian economies are now close to, or sometimes even below, the global average carbon intensity of about 0.4 kilogram per CO_2 per 2015 US dollars. Some economies nonetheless have carbon intensities substantially above the world average (e.g., Mongolia), and are thus exposed to the impacts of ambitious climate targets adopted worldwide. Even economies with relatively low carbon intensities may be outcompeted by firms from economies with less stringent climate targets.

The global objective to hold global temperature increase to well below 2°C above pre-industrial levels and pursue efforts to limit it to 1.5°C above pre-industrial levels, is to be achieved in part through the burden-sharing that the Paris Agreement contemplates. That instrument's NDCs are essential, with each party preparing, communicating, and maintaining successive commitments. They submit these declarations every 5 years to the United Nations Framework Convention on Climate Change (UNFCCC) Secretariat, with the next submissions being due in 2025. The Paris Agreement emphasizes a ratcheting up of ambition by which each successive NDC must represent progress over its predecessor. Adjustments to existing NDCs can be made at any time to enhance ambition. All Asia and Pacific countries had submitted NDCs by August 2021, and many submitted enhanced NDCs that increased their mitigation ambitions. Some NDCs include absolute emissions targets (e.g., the amount of emissions in 2030), while others use reductions below a baseline (e.g., a percentage reduction below an assumed emission pathway that would occur without additional climate measures) or an intensity target (e.g., emissions per unit of GDP). Some include one "unconditional" target, supplemented by a more ambitious "conditional" target that is contingent on assistance from the international community.

Figure 3.1: Carbon Intensity of Asia and Pacific Economies, 2012 vs. 2022
(total CO$_2$ emissions divided by gross domestic product in constant 2015 US dollars)

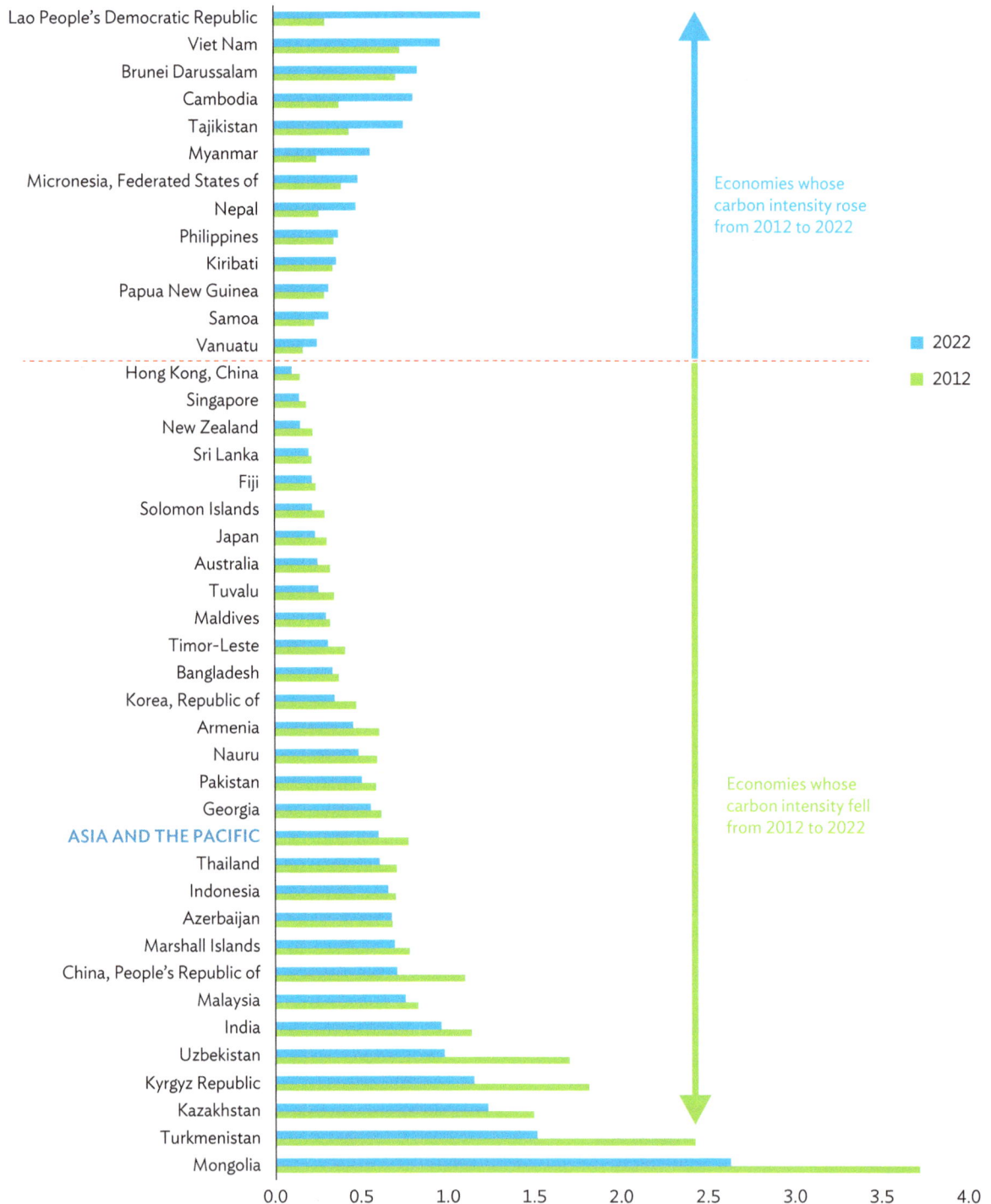

Economies whose carbon intensity rose from 2012 to 2022

Economies whose carbon intensity fell from 2012 to 2022

- 2022
- 2012

Notes: Total carbon dioxide (CO$_2$) emissions based on territorial emissions, which refer to the fossil CO$_2$ emissions produced within an economy, including exports but omitting imports. Economies Sorted First by Degree of 2012–2022 Progress and then by 2022 Levels.
Sources: Asian Development Bank calculations using data from Global Carbon Project. https://globalcarbonbudgetdata.org/latest-data.html and World Bank. World Development Indicators. https://databank.worldbank.org/ (accessed 31 May 2024).

Economies in Asia and the Pacific are also undertaking efforts to enhance their ability to adapt by improving waste and wastewater management; preventing or minimizing pollution; preserving natural resources; restoring ecosystems affected by air, water, and waste pollution; addressing noise pollution; conserving biodiversity and landscapes; conducting monitoring and assessment; implementing control measures; investing in research and development; promoting education and training; and enhancing information and communication related to environmental protection and resource management. SIDS, in particular, face special challenges in wastewater management, which was a leading topic at the Fourth Session of the United Nations Environment Assembly. A report issued by the United Nations Environment Programme (2019) found that reducing waste can save SIDS $35–$400 per ton, depending on the activity and the technologies used. As a way forward, the Asia and Pacific region region is increasingly adopting cleaner and more resource-efficient technologies and products that will help in improving resource productivity, reducing pollution intensity, and mitigating risks. These initiatives collectively contribute to building resilience against future environmental challenges.

Chapter 4

Aid for Trade and Climate Change

The Greening of Aid for Trade

With climate change being the most global of all challenges, countries in all regions and at all levels of development share a common interest in achieving the goals of the Paris Agreement. Donors and beneficiaries alike will benefit from the greening of AfT, with this program well-placed to ensure that trade is not just inclusive in its opportunities and results, but also sustainable for the foreseeable future. Figure 4.1 illustrates how the impacts of AfT translate down to the main stakeholders in an economy through the two interconnected layers of policies and broader conditions in the economy. The first layer consists of those related to trade, sectoral, climate, and labor, and the various programs of AfT work directly to change, directly or indirectly, these policies. These effects

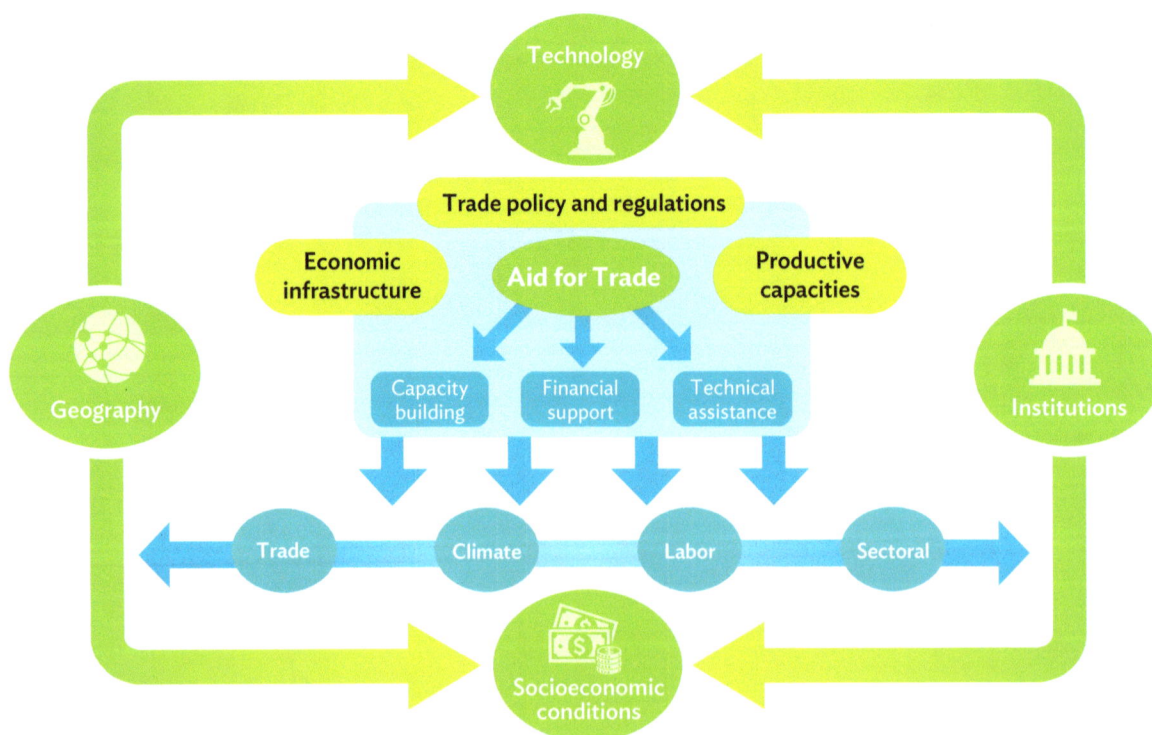

Figure 4.1: Aid for Trade and Climate Change Framework

Source: Authors.

are moderated by the preexisting set of institutions, technologies, geography, and socioeconomic conditions. Mainstreaming climate within AfT can best be disentangled by its increasing influence within the various components of AfT.

AfT's main component of technical assistance for trade policy and regulation is to assist economies in the management of their trade policy, as well as through trade facilitation, assisting with regional trade agreements, supporting multilateral trade agreements, and providing trade education and training. In the case of managing trade policy, there has been a concerted effort to incorporate climate considerations into trade-related legislation and regulations. This has included embedding sustainability criteria into the policy analysis and implementation of regional trade agreements (RTAs) and multilateral agreements dealing with such topics as technical barriers to trade and sanitary/phytosanitary standards.

AfT helps to harmonize trade-related climate standards and streamline customs procedures for environmentally friendly goods and technologies, aiming to improve import and export procedures for sustainable products and promote green trade. Digitalization is a central focus, designed to reduce the carbon footprint associated with trade activities and support the rapid dissemination of green technologies across borders. It assists economies in harmonizing the climate rules in RTAs, ensuring that sustainability remains a key component of economies' trade policies. Assistance is provided in drafting and incorporating environmental provisions in these agreements, aiming at addressing and integrating standards with an environmental focus. Other domains within these agreements, such as rules of origin and special and differential treatment, are increasingly viewed through an environmental lens before being negotiated.

AfT assists economies in participating in World Trade Organization (WTO) discussions on the environment, such as the Trade and Environmental Sustainability Structure Discussions (TESSD), the WTO Dialogue on Plastics Pollution (DPP) and the WTO Fossil Fuel Subsidy Reform (FFSR) initiative. While progress has been gradual, it has become an increasingly important agenda for the multilateral trading system (MTS) to hasten the integration of climate change considerations within its working processes.

AfT has also been active in educational activities to enhance the trade infrastructure of a country. It provides comprehensive training programs and education initiatives to train trade officials, business leaders, and other stakeholders to sensitize them on the MTS and the importance of integrating a climate agenda for sustainability. There is an increasing focus on clear programs to build capacity for green trade.

AfT is directly involved in economic infrastructure, in part through the provision, maintenance, and upgrading of transport, storage, and energy systems. These activities focus on green fuels and renewable energy so as to upgrade public transit and freight transport systems with cleaner fuels and greater energy efficiency. It also promotes the generation of renewable energy and expanding transportation networks to bring energy from the most efficient sources to where it is most needed. This has been coupled with a renewed focus on tackling unsustainable materials and the development of infrastructure for green energy storage. AfT programs have focused on reducing the carbon intensity of sectors by upgrading their equipment to be more energy-efficient, deploying carbon-capture and storage technologies, and enhancing their use of renewable energy.

Another AfT ambition is to build productive capacity in developing economies through a range of novel interventions. AfT has made finance a central focus of climate mainstreaming, working to upgrade banking and financial services to support green financial initiatives. For sectors still at the center of trade and climate (e.g., agriculture [see Box 4.1], forestry, ecotourism, and fishing), AfT advocates approaches that balance the exploitation of natural resources with efforts not to exhaust them. This is a way of ensuring that productive capacities are sustainable for local communities. Resource use and waste generation in the industry and mining sectors have historically contributed to a disproportionate level of greenhouse gases (GHGs), and a sustainability focus requires that they evolve with their counterparts in economies with greener economies.

Box 4.1: Mekong Case Study on Climate Adaptation in Agricultural Value Chains

The Greater Mekong Subregion (GMS) contains some of the largest corridors for agricultural trade between the People's Republic of China (PRC), the Lao People's Democratic Republic (Lao PDR), Myanmar, Viet Nam, and Cambodia. Rising demand in the PRC has contributed to a sharp rise in livestock production in the last 2 decades, and is expected to increase. This growth is accompanied by an expanding risk of disease caused by the cross-border movement of livestock. This risk is amplified by the presence of informality in the trade corridor and the relatively weaker existing systems for sanitary and phytosanitary compliance.

Livestock is one of the largest contributors to greenhouse gases, and one of the expected impacts of climate change is the likely increase in disaster outbreaks due to the negative physical effects of climate change on animals. The agriculture and livestock sectors remain especially vulnerable to climate change, and trade has the potential to amplify shocks. The rapid spread and widespread disruption caused by coronavirus disease (COVID-19) demonstrated the need to address any vulnerability in the agriculture sector, and the increasing complexity of agricultural supply chains further exacerbates the risk. This requires planning for adaptation and mitigation of the changes brought on by climate change.

An Asian Development Bank (ADB) project for the Lao PDR launched in 2022 with a funding of over $100 million addresses these vulnerabilities through a multipronged approach of filling infrastructural gaps, building capacity, and providing policy support in the areas of animal disease and food safety. The infrastructural component of this project includes the development of disease control zones (DCZs), which provide the ability to feed, inspect, and vaccinate livestock. In case of any disease outbreaks, they also provide quarantine facilities. The project also aims to fill gaps in infrastructure further down the chain with facilities for breeding, waste, slaughtering, processing, cold storage, and marketing.

The project aims to build capacity for government staff in epidemiology, livestock trade, and trade-certification systems. Systems are being introduced to provide for greater traceability and transparency in the sector, with both large and smallholders of livestock acquiring expertise for detecting, monitoring, and reporting livestock disasters. The project promotes inclusivity by working with smallholders and women to improve the harmonization of quality systems, formalize trade, introduce greater transparency, and encourage the private sector to invest in DCZ infrastructure.

All these interventions provide a good model for addressing the vulnerability at the nexus of trade and climate within the agriculture sector. The evolving impact of climate change on the sector is likely to affect trade (and vice versa in some cases). An inclusive approach centered on human health, disaster management, and common prosperity is required to guide both the mitigation and adaptation responses within this sector.

Further details of the program for the Lao PDR are from ADB's Greater Mekong Subregion Cross-Border Livestock Health and Value Chains Improvement Project. See also the proposals for Cambodia in Greater Mekong Subregion Cross-Border Livestock Health and Value Chains Improvement Project and for Myanmar in GMS Cross-Border Livestock Health and Value Chains Improvement Project.

Source: Authors.

AfT also aids economies in estimating and adapting to measures in export markets that aim to reduce carbon emissions, such as the Carbon Border Adjustment Mechanism (CBAM) of the European Union (EU). As discussed in Chapter 6, this measure seeks to level the playing field for EU domestic companies subject to carbon pricing with foreign competitors who are not subject to similar pricing. Other EU trade-related climate measures include the deforestation regulation and a range of climate-related export bans and prohibitions. AfT can help economies adapt to these changes and upgrade their infrastructure to minimize the impact of such measures.

Mainstreaming climate within trade remains a primary challenge for the MTS. The urgency of the effort is frequently brought up at multilateral climate conferences such as those held under the aegis of the United Nations Framework Convention on Climate Change (UNFCCC). As the WTO continues to advance its work in concert with these conferences and its members, AfT assists those that are least prepared to cope with these rapid changes.

Efforts to improve the environmental sustainability of trade will require significant investments in environmental law, institutions, and enforcement in developing economies (Birkbeck 2021). AfT support for cleaner energy production complements trade policies that facilitate access to new technologies and standards adherence and compliance. There are demands now for AfT to support trade-related adjustment because of green trade policy measures elsewhere.

This includes adjustment to climate-related trade measures as well as enhanced environmental compliance within supply chains (Monkelbaan, Keane, and Kaukab n.d.). Moreover, the unprecedented COVID-19 pandemic has emphasized the significance of addressing a wide range of risks to guarantee resilience in supply chains. The looming risk of climate change and its capacity to disrupt GVCs have become a primary concern globally.

Environmental Aid for Trade by Region and Subregion

Figures 4.2 and 4.3 illustrate the distribution of environmental AfT between regions and within Asia and the Pacific. Global commitments to environment-related[17] AfT had been experiencing a notable increase before declining in 2020, then rebounded with the recovery; it increased to $22.8 billion in 2022. The Asia and Pacific region emerged as the largest beneficiary of environment-related AfT commitments at the global level, reaching $11.3 billion in 2022. The share of Asia and the Pacific in total environment-related AfT commitments hovered between 36% and 61% over the 2002–2022 period and increased by 2% in the recovery phase. South Asia was the largest recipient of AfT commitments in environment-related activities between 2002 and 2022 with its share rising from 53% in 2019 to 74% in 2021 and declining to 57% in the recovery phase. Southeast Asia was the second-largest recipient of environment-related AfT commitments receiving 34% in 2022.

---

[17] Rio Convention Markers (Environment, Climate-Mitigation, Climate Adaptation, Biodiversity and Desertification), commonly referred as "climate-related Official Development Assistance (ODA)" activities, are scored as principal objective (climate change explicitly stated as the primary component in the activity), significant objective (climate-change stated as the secondary component in the activity), not targeted (screened as climate change activity but found not be targeted). An activity is defined as environment-related (with principal objective or significant objective) when it is intended to produce an improvement or includes specific action to integrate climate concerns through institution building and/or capacity development.

Figure 4.2: Environment-Related Aid for Trade by Region, 2002–2022

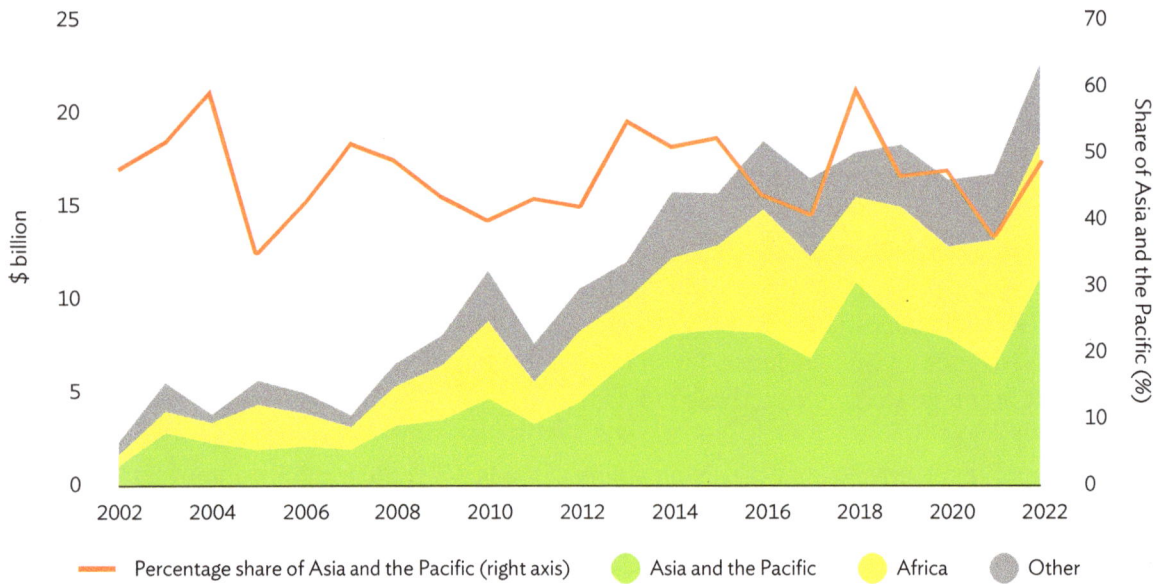

Note: "Other" includes America, Europe, and the Middle East. Total environment-related aid for trade is the sum of principal objective and significant objective aid for infrastructure, aid for building productive capacity, for trade policy and regulations, and trade-related adjustment.
Source: Asian Development Bank calculations using data from Organisation for Economic Co-operation and Development. Creditor Reporting System. Aid Activities Targeting Global Environmental Objectives. https://stats.oecd.org/Index. aspx?DataSetCode=RIOMARKERS#.

Figure 4.3: Environment-Related Aid for Trade by Subregion, 2002–2022
($ billion)

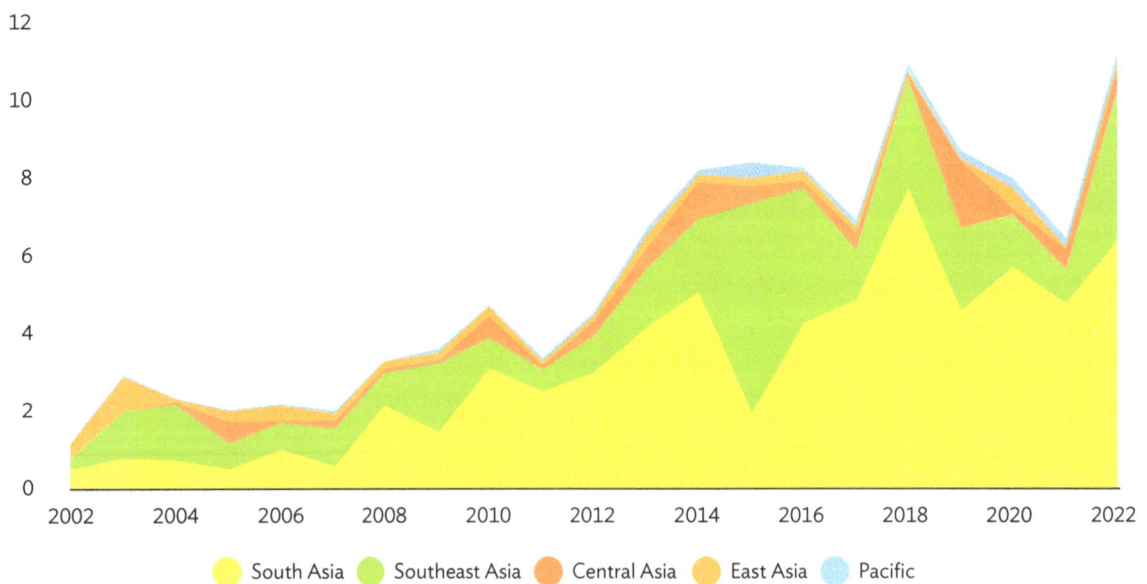

Source: Asian Development Bank calculations using data from Organisation for Economic Co-operation and Development. Creditor Reporting System. Aid Activities Targeting Global Environmental Objectives. https://stats.oecd.org/Index. aspx?DataSetCode=RIOMARKERS#.

Central Asia and the Pacific's shares increased marginally in the recovery phase, respectively, from 2% and 2.5% in 2020 to 8% and 3.3% in 2021, and declined again to 5% and 2.5% in 2022. While the share of Southeast Asia had been declining since 2016, it rebounded to 34% in 2022 from 13% in 2021. Since 2007, East Asia has experienced a significant decline in the AfT commitments related to environment.

Asia and the Pacific predominantly received AfT support in climate mitigation-related activities. Support was relatively over the period for climate adaptation-related activities for bolstering adaptive capabilities and resilience. Asia and the Pacific was the largest recipient of climate mitigation-related[18] AfT commitments in 2002–2022, and Africa was the largest recipient of climate adaptation-related[19] AfT commitments in the same period (Figure 4.4). This indicates that AfT can be further harnessed to build climate-resilient infrastructure, foster long-term development, promote post-pandemic recovery, and help the region pursue climate change mitigation and adaptation policies while catalyzing sustainable trade competitiveness.

Figure 4.4: Distribution of Climate Adaptation and Mitigation Aid for Trade, by Region, 2002–2022

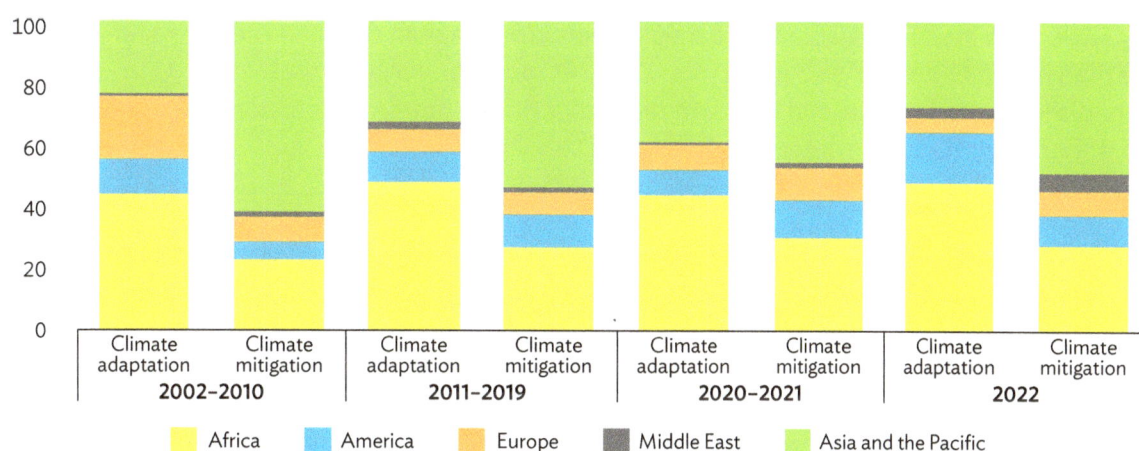

Notes:
(1)   Total climate adaptation-related aid for trade is the sum of principal objective and significant objective aid for infrastructure, aid for building productive capacity, trade policy and regulations, and trade-related adjustment.
(2)   Total climate mitigation-related aid for trade is the sum of principal objective and significant objective aid for infrastructure, aid for building productive capacity, trade policy and regulations, and trade-related adjustment.
(3)   9-year and 2-year averages are calculated using constant 2021 United States dollar.
Source: Asian Development Bank calculations using data from Organisation for Economic Co-operation and Development. Creditor Reporting System. Aid Activities Targeting Global Environmental Objectives. https://stats.oecd.org/Index. aspx?DataSetCode=RIOMARKERS#.

[18]   Climate mitigation-related activity (with principal objective or significant objective) contributes to the objective of stabilization of greenhouse gas (GHG) concentrations in the atmosphere at a level that would prevent harmful anthropogenic interference with the climate system by promoting efforts to reduce or control GHG emissions or to enhance GHG sequestration.
[19]   Climate adaptation-related activity (with principal objective or significant objective) intends to reduce the vulnerability of human or natural systems to the impacts of climate change and associated risks, by either maintaining or bolstering adaptive capabilities and resilience.

AfT's commitment to address climate adaptation and climate mitigation increased for all Asian subregions, with a noticeable spike during the pandemic (Figure 4.5). In the recovery phase, Southeast Asia (51%) has been the largest recipient of climate adaptation-related AfT commitments, followed by South Asia (25%). In 2022, South Asia was the largest recipient of climate mitigation-related AfT commitments (60%), followed by Southeast Asia (32%). Although the average share of Central Asia and the Pacific region were the lowest for both climate adaptation-related and climate mitigation-related activities, the average share for the Pacific region in climate adaptation-related activities increased from 5.5% in 2002–2010 to 10.2% in 2022. The average share for Central Asia in climate adaptation-related activities increased from 6% in 2002–2010 to 14% in 2022. The subregion began receiving climate-related AfT commitments in climate adaptation only after 2010, indicating that efforts are required to accelerate subregional support.

As may be seen in Table 4.1, 7 of the top 10 recipient economies of environment-related AfT commitments were located in South Asia and Southeast Asia, with India as the largest recipient. Six of the bottom 10 economies were in the Pacific subregion. When viewed in per capita terms, however, Pacific economies have the highest environment-related AfT commitments. AfT accounted for more than 70% of total environment-related official development assistance (ODA) commitments in India, Bangladesh, and the Philippines; more than 65% in Azerbaijan and Palau; and more than half in two East Asian economies (the PRC and Mongolia), Uzbekistan in Central Asia, Cambodia in Southeast Asia, and Nauru in the Pacific. In the bottom 10 economies, AfT accounted for less than 30% of total environment-related ODA.

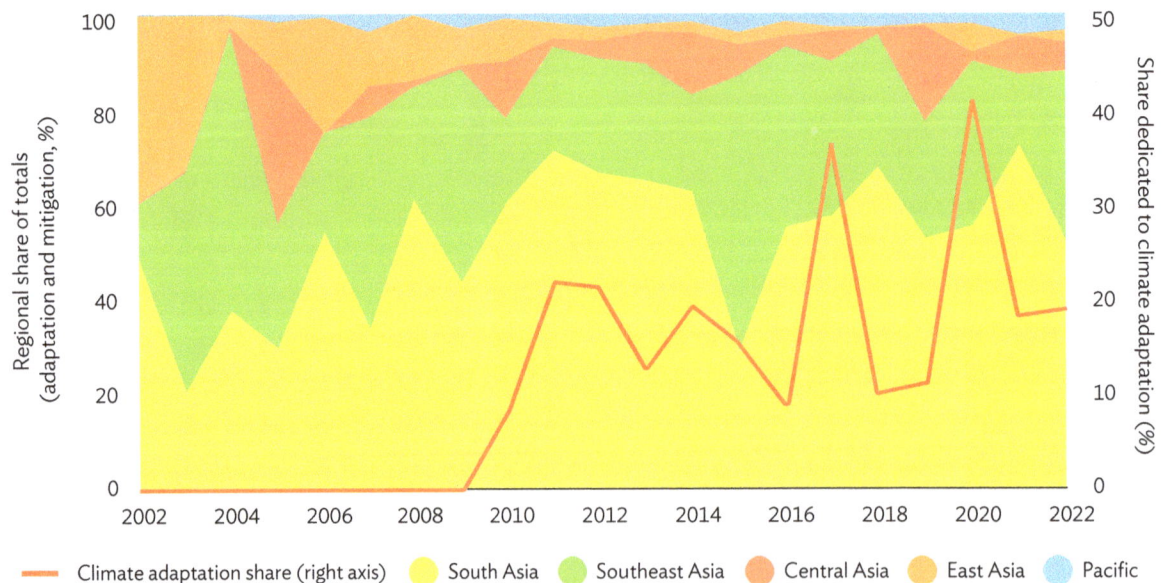

Figure 4.5: Distribution of Climate Adaptation and Mitigation Aid for Trade for Asia and the Pacific, 2002–2022

Source: Asian Development Bank calculations using data from Organisation for Economic Co-operation and Development. Creditor Reporting System. Aid Activities Targeting Global Environmental Objectives. https://stats.oecd.org/Index. aspx?DataSetCode=RIOMARKERS#.

Table 4.1: Top 10 and Bottom 10 Environment-Related Aid for Trade, 2020–2022
(annual averages)

Total Environment-Related AfT ($ million)		Per Capita ($)		% of Total Environment-Related ODA	
Top 10		**Top 10**		**Top 10**	
India	3,612.25	Palau	444.77	India	78.87
Bangladesh	1,757.32	Niue	205.86	Bangladesh	73.87
Philippines	948.39	Nauru	184.03	Philippines	73.64
Indonesia	299.47	Kiribati	72.41	Azerbaijan	66.47
Viet Nam	265.34	Marshall Islands	49.04	Palau	65.52
Cambodia	236.21	Vanuatu	47.91	PRC	58.83
Uzbekistan	225.51	Tonga	47.02	Mongolia	55.81
Myanmar	214.04	Solomon Islands	40.31	Cambodia	55.68
PRC	209.32	Samoa	24.36	Nauru	55.20
Papua New Guinea	133.54	Fiji	22.67	Uzbekistan	54.83
Bottom 10		**Bottom 10**		**Bottom 10**	
Turkmenistan	0.05	Turkmenistan	0.01	Turkmenistan	1.95
Niue	0.35	Malaysia	0.09	Georgia	16.65
FSM	0.74	PRC	0.15	FSM	17.74
Maldives	1.06	Kazakhstan	0.18	Samoa	19.05
Marshall Islands	2.08	Thailand	0.28	Afghanistan	21.26
Nauru	2.30	Pakistan	0.49	Vanuatu	22.55
Malaysia	2.95	Sri Lanka	0.98	Tonga	25.87
Kazakhstan	3.50	Indonesia	1.09	Bhutan	28.88
Tonga	4.99	Afghanistan	1.61	Malaysia	29.72
Samoa	5.33	Azerbaijan	1.65	Sri Lanka	29.82

AfT = Aid for Trade, PRC = People's Republic of China, FSM = Federated States of Micronesia, ODA = official development assistance.
Note: 3-year averages calculated using 2021 constant United States dollars.
Sources: Asian Development Bank (ADB) calculations using data from Organisation for Economic Co-operation and Development. Creditor Reporting System. Aid Activities Targeting Global Environmental Objectives. https://stats.oecd.org/Index.aspx?DataSetCode=RIOMARKERS#; World Bank. World Development Indicators, https://databank.worldbank.org/ (accessed 31 January 2024); for the population of Niue and the Cook Islands: ADB. Key Indicators for Asia and the Pacific 2023. https://www.adb.org/publications/keyindicators-asia-and-pacific-2023 (accessed 31 January 2024).

Environmental Aid for Trade by Purpose and Sector

AfT's policy initiatives aim to assist all developing economies, particularly the least developed countries, to integrate into the multilateral trading system. That objective is made more complicated by the simultaneous demands to address climate change, but these need not be seen as mutually exclusive objectives. Environmental sustainability is emerging as a pivotal aspect of trade policy for predicating climate-resilient pathways and propelling the global economy toward a greener trajectory.

When economies integrate environmental considerations in AfT activities they enhance their adaptation and resilience to climate change, facilitating a sustainable recovery and promoting export diversification and competitiveness. AfT can facilitate the deployment of renewable energy and encourage the adoption and promotion of cleaner and more efficient technologies. Additionally, AfT can assist in sustainable infrastructure development by incorporating comprehensive and integrated components for environmental protection and management. AfT can play a complementary role in enhancing the capacity to seize new green market access opportunities by embracing sustainability standards and enhancing quality infrastructure. AfT in trade policy and regulation can complement trade policies and agreements that safeguard biodiversity and ecosystems. AfT can also help in enhancing the capacity to negotiate and implement trade agreements concerning the exchange of green goods, services, and technologies necessary for climate adaptation, mitigation, and disaster preparedness and response. Moreover, AfT could help in formulating and executing policies aimed at enhancing sustainability within global value chains and facilitating integration into these chains.

The region's prioritization of environmental considerations is clear from the evolution of AfT flows by purpose. Figure 4.6 shows that the economic infrastructure sector received the majority of environment-related AfT commitments, increasing from $2 billion annually during 2002–2010 to $6.3 billion in 2011–2019, then declining to $6 billion with the pandemic and

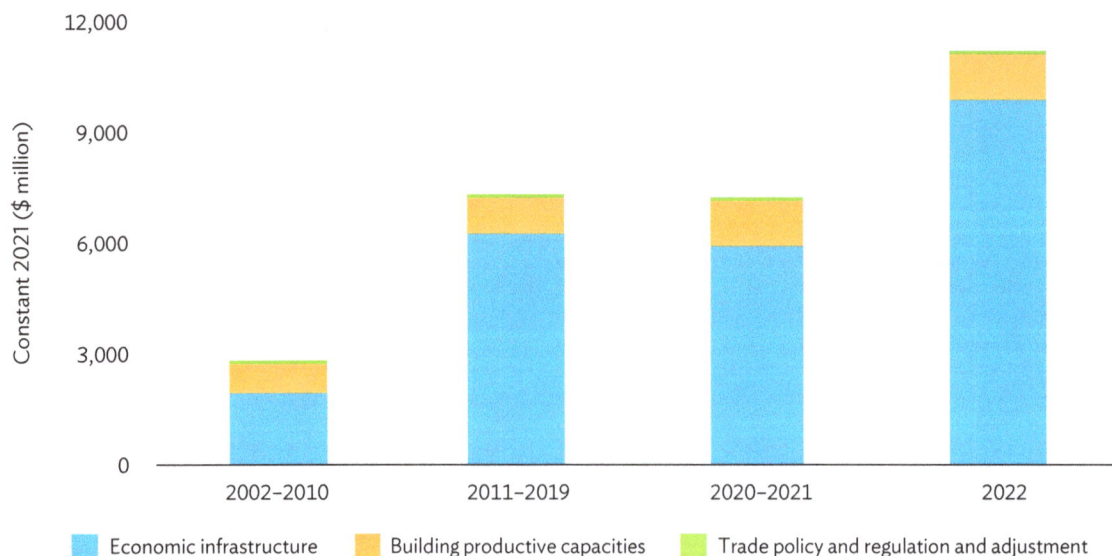

Figure 4.6: Value of Environment-Related Aid for Trade in Asia and the Pacific, by Purpose, 2002–2022

Notes:
(1) Environment-related aid for trade for economic infrastructure, building productive capacities and trade policy and regulation and trade-related adjustment is the sum of principal objective and significant objective.
(2) 9-year and 2-year averages are calculated using constant 2021 United States dollars.
Source: Asian Development Bank calculations using data from Organisation for Economic Co-operation and Development. Creditor Reporting System. Aid Activities Targeting Global Environmental Objectives. https://stats.oecd.org/Index. aspx?DataSetCode=RIOMARKERS#.

rebounding to $10 billion in the recovery. Building productive capacity was the second-largest broad AfT sector receiving environment-related AfT, increasing consistently even during the pandemic from $0.7 billion between 2002 and 2010 to $1.26 billion in 2022. On the other hand, environment-related AfT support to trade policy and regulation and adjustment activities declined from $34 million in 2002–2012 to $14 million in 2020–2021 and further declined to $11 million in 2022. However, $4.8 billion AfT commitments were made toward economic infrastructure activities supporting the environment as a principal objective (climate change was explicitly stated as the primary component in the activity) during 2020–2022 (Table 4.2). The rise of environment-related AfT commitments in economic infrastructure activities could be attributed to the changing global order of climate actions and mitigation with the establishment of the Paris Agreement and several proactive climate change mitigation and adaptation measures at the national levels.

As shown in Table 4.2, productive capacity activities supporting environment received only 3% of the AfT commitments as a principal objective and 6% as a significant objective. Although production activities such as agriculture, forestry, fishing, industry, mineral resources, and mining are essential to preserving biodiversity and landscapes, only about 13% of AfT commitments were directed toward these activities. Increasing AfT support in production activities supporting environment can play a complementary role in enhancing capacity to seize new "green" market access opportunities by embracing sustainability standards and enhancing quality infrastructure. Most of the AfT commitments supporting environment in trade policy and regulation activities were screened but not targeted during 2002–2022. Moreover, the AfT commitments supporting trade policy and regulation activities as principal and significant objectives have drastically reduced since 2008–2010.

Economic infrastructure with significant potential for reducing GHG emissions in road, rail, water and air transport, and energy generation and supply sectors received AfT support of $10 billion in climate mitigation-related activities in 2022. Building productive capacity sector received AfT support of $0.7 billion in climate adaptation-related activities for bolstering adaptive capabilities and resilience in agriculture, forestry, and fishing in 2022, and trade policy and regulations and trade-related adjustment received about $3 million in both climate mitigation and climate adaptation-related activities in 2022.

Economic infrastructure and trade policy and regulations and trade-related adjustment received AfT support in climate mitigation-related activities with significant potential for reducing GHG emissions in 2002–2022 (Figure 4.7). The impact of the pandemic can be seen at the sector level as well. The average share of climate mitigation-related AfT commitments supporting economic infrastructure declined from 92.4% during 2011–2019 to 71.4% during 2020–2021 and rebounded to 88.6% in 2022. Similarly, climate adaptation-related AfT commitments supporting building productive capacity sector rebounded from 59.5% during 2020–2021 to 62.2% in 2022. For trade policy and regulation and trade-related adjustment, the average share of climate mitigation-related AfT commitments seem to decline consistently from 69.5% during 2011–2019 to 49.6% in 2022.

Table 4.2: Values and Shares of Environment-Related Aid for Trade in Asia and the Pacific, by Purpose, 2002–2022

(value in $ million and $ billion of constant 2021 United States dollars)

	Economic Infrastructure and Services				Production				Trade Policy and Regulations			
	Significant	Principal	Not Targeted	Not Screened	Significant	Principal	Not Targeted	Not Screened	Significant	Principal	Not Targeted	Not Screened
	3-Year Total Value ($ billion)				**3-Year Total Value ($ billion)**				**3-Year Total Value ($ million)**			
2002–2004	4.3	0.7	7.8	0.7	0.5	1.0	3.0	1.5	21.4	0.4	210.3	57.2
2005–2007	4.0	0.1	10.1	0.5	1.0	1.1	6.0	0.7	62.7	2.6	201.6	12.7
2008–2010	7.9	1.1	12.7	1.4	1.4	1.1	5.0	1.9	196.7	3.0	372.1	30.1
2011–2013	9.6	1.8	12.8	1.2	2.1	1.1	5.4	0.5	204.9	2.8	353.9	33.0
2014–2016	13.1	8.7	14.5	1.1	2.0	1.2	4.6	1.1	128.5	18.5	330.5	18.0
2017–2019	20.0	3.7	12.1	1.1	1.9	1.1	5.5	0.3	100.1	8.5	751.0	8.4
2020–2022	17.3	4.8	8.6	1.6	2.5	1.3	3.6	0.5	37.7	15.3	188.5	3.7
	Share of 3-Year Total (%)				**Share of 3-Year Total (%)**				**Share of 3-Year Total (%)**			
2002–2004	21.8	3.6	39.5	3.5	2.4	5.1	15.2	7.5	0.1	<0.1	1.1	0.3
2005–2007	16.8	0.6	42.5	2.0	4.1	4.7	25.2	2.9	0.3	<0.1	0.8	0.1
2008–2010	23.8	3.3	38.3	4.2	4.3	3.3	15.1	5.8	0.6	<0.1	1.1	0.1
2011–2013	27.3	5.0	36.5	3.5	5.9	3.2	15.4	1.5	0.6	<0.1	1.0	0.1
2014–2016	28.0	18.5	30.9	2.4	4.2	2.6	9.9	2.3	0.3	<0.1	0.7	<0.1
2017–2019	43.0	7.9	26.0	2.4	4.0	2.4	11.8	0.6	0.2	<0.1	1.6	<0.1
2020–2022	43.0	11.8	21.2	4.0	6.1	3.1	8.9	1.3	0.1	<0.1	0.5	<0.1

Source: Asian Development Bank calculations using data from Organisation for Economic Co-operation and Development. Creditor Reporting System. Aid Activities Targeting Global Environmental Objectives. https://stats.oecd.org/Index.aspx?DataSetCode=RIOMARKERS#.

Figure 4.7: Asia and Pacific Climate Adaptation and Mitigation Aid for Trade, by Purpose, 2002–2022
(percentage share)

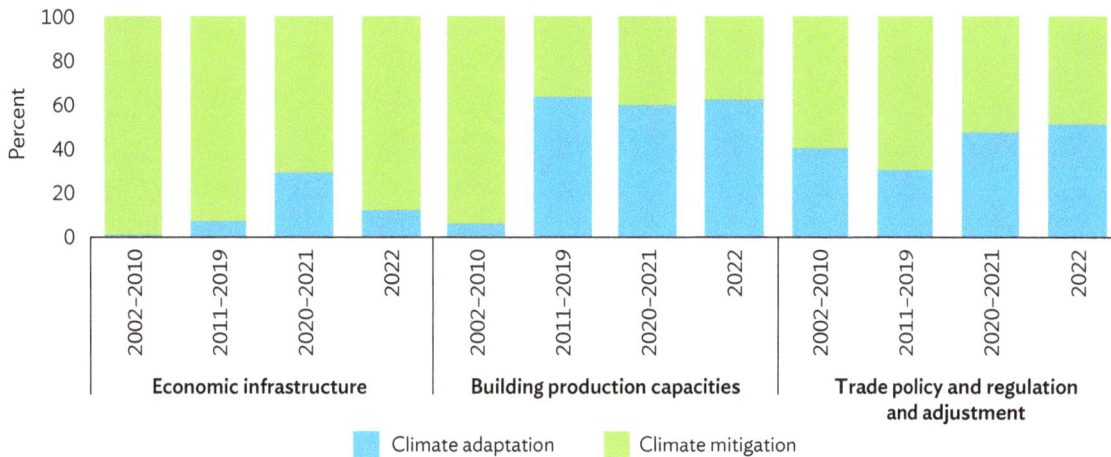

Notes:
(1) Climate adaptation-related aid for trade is the sum of principal objective and significant objective aid for infrastructure, building productive capacity, trade policy and regulations, and trade-related adjustment.
(2) Climate mitigation-related aid for trade is the sum of principal objective and significant objective aid for infrastructure, building productive capacity, trade policy and regulations, and trade-related adjustment.
(3) 9-year and 2-year averages are calculated in constant 2021 United States dollars.
Source: Asian Development Bank calculations using data from Organisation for Economic Co-operation and Development. Creditor Reporting System. Aid Activities Targeting Global Environmental Objectives. https://stats.oecd.org/Index.aspx?DataSetCode=RIOMARKERS#.

Support from AfT will also be crucial in facilitating structural changes that might be necessary to decarbonize sectors. The transport and storage sector under economic infrastructure was the primary recipient of AfT commitments pertaining to environment between 2002 and 2021, with the average share consistently rising from 40% to 67% by 2020–2021 and further rising to 70% in the recovery phase (Figure 4.8). The energy sector under economic infrastructure was the second-largest recipient of environment-related AfT commitments with a 19% share in 2022 (rebounding from 14.4% during the pandemic). Within the GHG-intensive energy sector there is a discernible trend toward increasing support for renewable energies. The average share of AfT commitments in renewable energy sources in total renewable energy aid rose to 84% in 2022 from about 50% during 2020, reflecting increasing support of AfT commitments toward mitigating climate change in the recovery phase (Figure 4.9).

Figure 4.8: Distribution of Environment-Related Aid for Trade by Sector, 2002–2022
(percentage share)

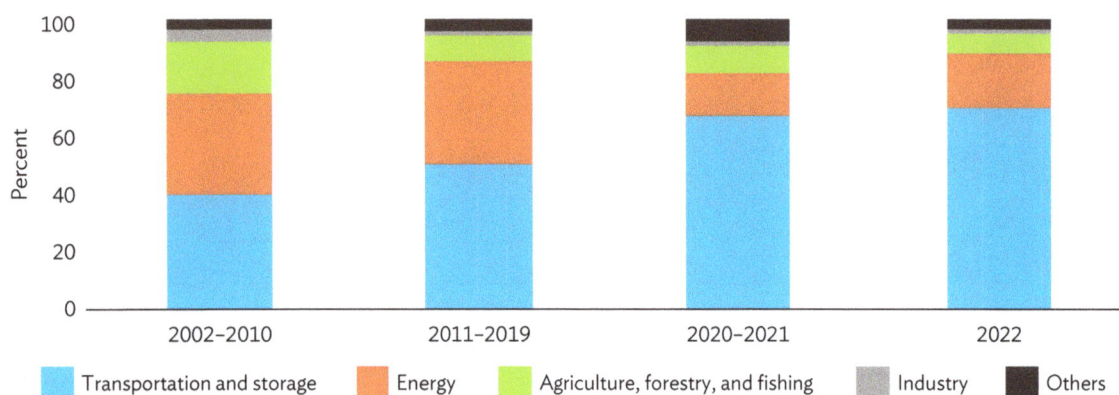

Notes:
(1)   Environment-related aid for trade is the sum of principal objective and significant objective for transport and storage, energy, agriculture, forestry and fishing, and industry subsector.
(2)   9-year and 2-year averages are calculated using constant 2021 United States dollars.
Source: Asian Development Bank calculations using data from Organisation for Economic Co-operation and Development. Creditor Reporting System. Aid Activities Targeting Global Environmental Objectives. https://stats.oecd.org/Index. aspx?DataSetCode=RIOMARKERS#.

Figure 4.9: Share of Environment-Related Aid for Trade by Renewable and Nonrenewable Energy Sectors, 2002–2022
(percentage shares calculated using constant 2021 United States dollars)

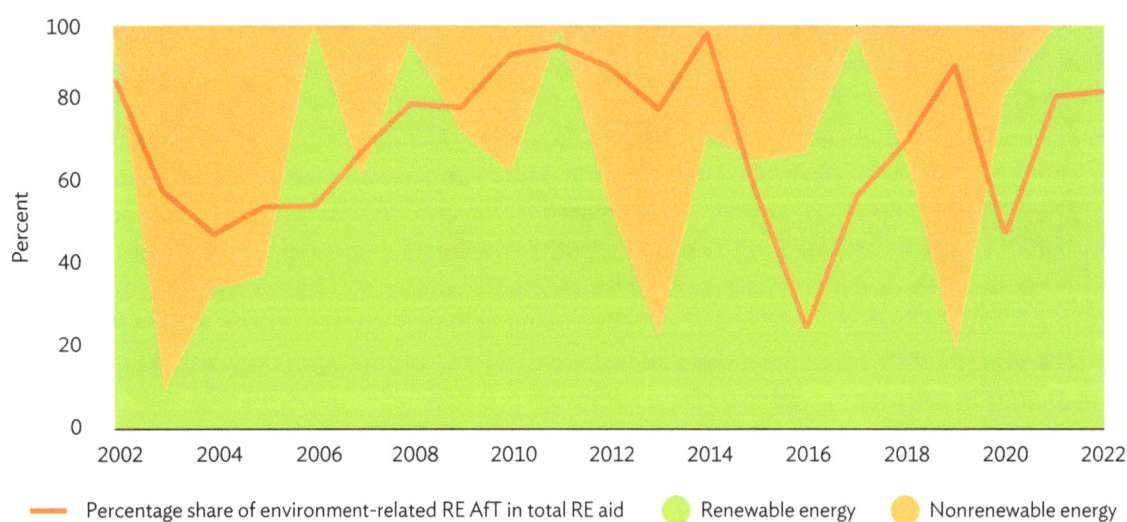

AfT = Aid for Trade, RE = renewable energy.
Note: Environment-related AfT for renewable and nonrenewable energy sector is the sum of principal objective and significant objective.
Source: Asian Development Bank calculations using data from Organisation for Economic Co-operation and Development. Creditor Reporting System. Aid Activities Targeting Global Environmental Objectives. https://stats.oecd.org/Index. aspx?DataSetCode=RIOMARKERS#.

Most AfT commitments in the transport and storage, energy and industry sectors are rooted in climate mitigation-related activities with significant potential for reducing GHG emissions. Climate adaptation-related AfT commitments predominate in the agriculture, forestry, and fishing sector, which are closely intertwined with nature. The average share of climate mitigation-related AfT support in the transport and storage and industry sectors rebounded in 2022 to 87% and 82%, respectively, but not for the energy sector (Figure 4.10). The average share of climate adaptation-related AfT support rose to 73% for the agriculture, forestry and fishing sector in the recovery phase. ADB has also established various climate commitments and ambitions to support the developing economies that are threatened by climate change at the regional level (see Box 4.2).

AfT can be a building block for climate targets, sustainable export diversification, and trade competitiveness, thus raising the region's capacity to attain Sustainable Development Goal (SDG) targets. It can help economies reach emissions-abatement targets, enabling their transition to competitive, low-carbon economies. AfT can facilitate development and the adoption of green technologies, enhance access to a range of mitigation and adaptation technologies, mitigating vulnerability to sudden disruptions and extraordinary challenges unleashed by COVID-19. AfT can help economies formulate, foster prudent climate change policies and inclusive, resilient, and sustainable trade policy.

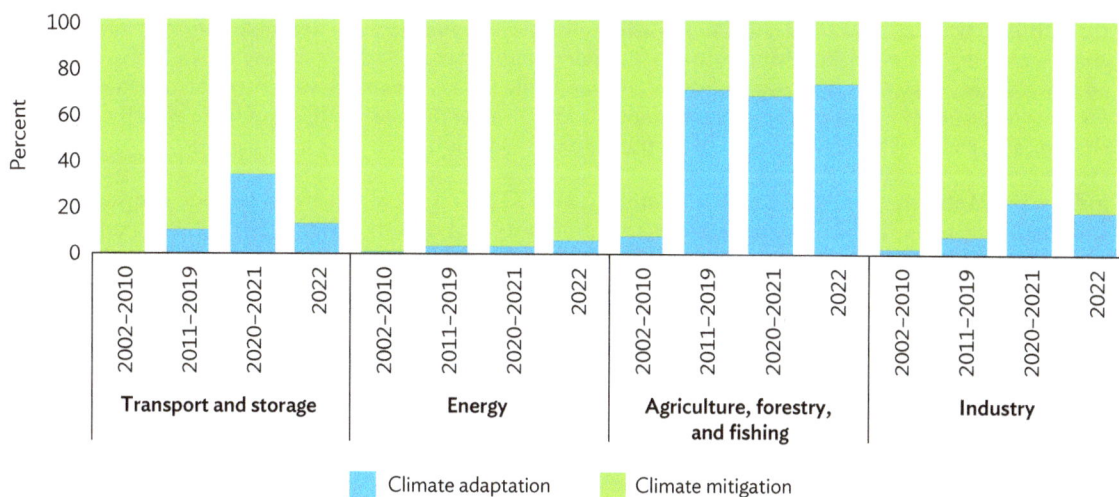

Figure 4.10: Asia and Pacific Climate Adaptation and Mitigation Aid for Trade by Sector, 2002–2022
(percentage shares calculated using constant 2021 United States dollars)

AfT = Aid for Trade.
Notes:
(1) Climate adaptation-related AfT is the sum of principal objective and significant objective aid for infrastructure, building productive capacity, trade policy and regulations, and trade-related adjustment.
(2) Climate mitigation-related AfT is the sum of principal objective and significant objective aid for infrastructure, building productive capacity, trade policy and regulations, and trade-related adjustment.
Source: ADB calculations using data from Organisation for Economic Co-operation and Development. Creditor Reporting System. Aid Activities Targeting Global Environmental Objectives. https://stats.oecd.org/Index.aspx?DataSetCode=RIOMARKERS#.

Box 4.2: Regional Cooperative Initiatives at the Trade/Climate Nexus

Climate change threatens the viability of many economic sectors that the Asian Development Bank (ADB) supports, a challenge best dealt with at the regional level. ADB's climate commitments and ambitions include mobilizing $80 billion in climate finance from its own resources between 2019 and 2030, toward a total target of $100 billion; disbursing $9 billion in climate adaptation finance from 2019 to 2024; supporting private initiatives with $12 billion in cumulative climate finance from own resources between 2019 and 2030; and ensuring that at least 65% of its operations contribute to climate change mitigation and/or adaptation by 2024. ADB also aims to align with the Paris Agreement's mitigation and adaptation objectives . Four projects that stand out are as follows.

Central Asia Regional Economic Cooperation (CAREC) Program. This program integrates climate change into its strategic framework. The regional vision adopted in 2023 has three main objectives: mitigating climate change by achieving carbon neutrality and reducing greenhouse gas emissions in such sectors as energy, transport, agriculture, and urban development; adapting to climate change through disaster risk reduction, climate adaptation financing, and natural resource conservation; and promoting cross-border cooperation by sharing technologies, knowledge, and experiences in climate action. The vision emphasizes the importance of sectors like transport, transit, and trade, which are vital to today's climate change discussion. ADB is preparing to establish the Climate and Sustainability Project Preparatory Fund to address infrastructure and climate finance gaps in CAREC economies.

South Asia Subregional Economic Cooperation (SASEC). This project aims to help one of the fastest-growing regions of Asia to leverage its momentum over the years 2016–2025. It will contribute to climate-change mitigation through *inter alia* diversification of energy generation sources, to ensure that the available energy trade infrastructure is upgraded. A shift to renewable sources, aided by energy transportation corridors, can help reduce the carbon intensity of many industries in the region.

Brunei Darussalam-Indonesia-Malaysia-Philippines East ASEAN Growth Area (BIMP-EAGA). The program will mobilize private sector investments to reduce barriers to the cross-border movement of people, goods, and services. The $38.9 billion program aims to improve sustainability within certain sectors (ecotourism) while also greening cities and assisting micro, small, and medium-sized enterprises in adopting green technologies toward improving both climate change mitigation and adaptation measures. It also focuses on power interconnections between countries, and improving the sustainable development of industries where the countries already have a comparative advantage and are vulnerable to the effects of trade and climate change (e.g., green manufacturing, agro-industry, fisheries, and tourism).

Indonesia-Malaysia-Thailand Growth Triangle (IMT-GT). This initiative aims to upgrade mitigation and adaptation policies while focusing on economic prosperity through trade. The 2017–2021 component of the initiative had a strategic focus for its 2036 plan on trade and investment facilitation, agriculture, and agro-based industry and the environment. The stress on the environment aims to promote renewable energy, sustainable management of natural resources, and to make cities less carbon-intensive while promoting green mobility. It also has a sharp focus on ensuring that cross-border agricultural value chains are made more environmentally friendly and sustainable.

Source: Authors.

Chapter 5

Environmental Trade Policy Instruments and Cooperation

Introduction

Climate change has been a leading issue in the international community for the past generation. Nearly all countries have committed to the ambition of the Paris Agreement, which seeks to limit global greenhouse gas (GHG) emissions to well below 2°C above pre-industrial levels, and to pursue efforts to limit the temperature increase to 1.5°C levels. The issue is being deliberated not just in dedicated United Nations conferences, as countries also deal with it—and with one another—in a wide range of regional, plurilateral, and multilateral settings.

Engaging in high-quality preferential trade agreements can support the global transition toward green, resilient, and sustainable growth through enhanced market access and more diversified environmental goods and services trade. Free trade agreements with provisions that substantially eliminate trade and investment barriers play a crucial role in enhancing production and consumption of environmental goods and services. Liberalized trade also facilitates firms' access to lower-priced inputs and clean technologies that are crucial in the decarbonization of global value chains. This is expected to improve the limited capacity among developing economies to spur innovation in low-carbon technologies, and enhance their competitiveness leveraging on green, sustainable growth (Kaufman et al. 2023).

Fostering partnerships through trade agreements can be instrumental in diversifying market sources and destinations for environmental goods and services. At a time when economies globally are challenged by persistent and overlapping crises, diversification helps economies manage supply and price volatilities resulting from external shocks and provides a more stable path for sustained economic growth. The recent pandemic experience demonstrated how supply chain disruptions jeopardized the availability of necessities and services. Russia's war in Ukraine exacerbated export restrictions, resulting in greater scarcity on agricultural and energy markets among importing regions, and an upward drift in commodity prices (ADB 2023d). ADB's most recent Asian Economic Integration Report looks into food security and found that the share of restrictive interventions covering Asia's food trade has increased since the pandemic, impeding the region's potential to build a resilient and stable regional food supplies (ADB 2024). Diversifying input sources or production areas, especially for essential goods, decreases economies' susceptibility to overlapping supply disruptions. International Monetary Fund (2022) simulations show that in the presence of supply shocks, increasing the geographic diversification of input sources and increasing the substitutability of inputs across sources in different economies reduces GDP losses by almost half and GDP volatility by 5%.

As part of a holistic and coordinated approach, trade diversification can effectively contribute to enhancing environmental sustainability. If supported by appropriate government interventions and regulations, diversifying trade and investment can promote access to less resource-intensive and more environment-friendly products, thereby inducing the shift to less pollution-driven production methods (Ali et al. 2022; Letchumanan and Kodama 2000). Shahzad et al. (2020) found that export product diversification encourages the creation of higher value-added products with lower carbon footprints, significantly reducing CO_2 emissions. In this regard, trade diversification, by strengthening value chain linkages and promoting economic sophistication, can serve as an important strategy to reduce emissions.

The State of Play in International Negotiations

One major divide concerns the use of unilateral measures such as border carbon adjustments (BCAs). The People's Republic of China (PRC) and India, backed by others such as Brazil and South Africa, proposed that unilateral trade measures be discussed at COP28.[20] Although the issue did not make it onto the agenda, the conference underlined for public and private sectors the importance of integrating climate considerations into economic and financial decision-making. It also provided a strong signal to the global community that current actions alone will not achieve the global temperature targets.

The World Trade Organization (WTO) plays a pivotal role in green trade, encouraging environmentally sustainable practices across its member economies. Its involvement in green trade primarily revolves around framing trade policies that incentivize environmentally friendly products and services, reducing trade barriers for green technologies, and ensuring that environmental objectives are integrated in the broader trade framework. It also handles trade disputes that may arise when countries use trade-related instruments in pursuit of their environmental objectives.

The 1994 Marrakesh Agreement establishing the WTO enshrined the protection and preservation of the environment as one objective of the multilateral trading system (WTO 1994a). The conclusion of the Uruguay Round negotiations (1986–1994) launched a comprehensive work program on trade, environment, and sustainable development (WTO 1994b). It also adopted the ministerial Decision on Trade and the Environment, which called for the establishment of a Committee on Trade and Environment (CTE), and the Decision on Trade in Services and the Environment. The decisions mandated CTE to identify the relationship between trade and environmental measures in promoting sustainable development and to make recommendations in enhancing their positive interaction while preserving the open, equitable, and nondiscriminatory nature of the multilateral trading system (MTS) (WTO 1994c; WTO 1994d). The Doha Round that began in 2001 sought to enhance this mutual supportiveness by negotiating the reduction or elimination of barriers to trade in environmental goods and services (EGS) (WTO 2001).

The Committee on Trade and the Environment held its first session on the energy transition in 2023. No links have yet been made to the UNFCCC Just Energy Transition Partnerships—which don't currently include any countries in the Asia and Pacific region. Plurilateral initiatives are grappling with the issues of fossil fuel subsidies at the WTO, where progress remains slow.

---

[20] The debates over these proposals are documented at unfccc.int/sites/default/files/resource/COP2_BASIC-Agenda proposal.pdf.

It is notable that the 13th WTO ministerial conference (MC13) in early 2024 secured a Ministerial Declaration on Technical Barriers to Trade which refers to climate change and sustainability issues. In addition, three WTO trade and environment plurilateral initiatives, TESSD, DPP, and FFSR issued MC13 statements.[21] However, MC13 also clearly identified the divide between economies that seek greater policy coordination and consideration of new issues, compared to others who feel that the existing multilateral framework is sufficient. Some members of the WTO remain opposed to its engagement on climate-related trade issues, while others such as Bangladesh, Indonesia, and Kazakhstan are pushing for the WTO to address these challenges (as exemplified by the Ministerial Declaration on the Contribution of the Multilateral Trading System to Tackle Environmental Challenges).[22]

Market Access for Environmental Goods and Services

EGS trade offers significant positive externalities. By boosting this commerce, developing member countries (DMCs) can better cope with the long-term effects of climate change and the policy responses of their foreign partners. Trade can facilitate the advancement, availability, and utilization of environmental technologies, thus mitigating GHG emissions by stimulating innovation and driving down the costs of low-carbon technologies through efficiency and economies of scale. EGS trade also allows economies to adapt environmental technologies to their local requirements, enhance the sustainability provisions of trade agreements, foster partnerships, and facilitate dialogues within the international community to raise awareness and secure much-needed financing, investments, and technologies for rebuilding a more resilient trading framework (UNEP 2020).

Although one might suppose that the definition of environmental goods is largely an objective and technical matter, with more statistical than substantive impact,[23] quite the opposite is true: The definition of environmental goods and services with the inclusion of adapted goods, specifically tailored to be more environmentally friendly or cleaner, and whose utilization promotes environmental protection or resource management, is critical for Asia and the Pacific (APEC 2022). For example, climate-smart water management systems and digital agricultural services disseminating climate information can be critical adaptation investments incorporated into agriculture, food, and natural resource projects. Technology transfers can facilitate manufacturing scaleups and innovation in multiple contexts. Promoting additional products to incentivize climate change adaptation and mitigation could assist economies in intensifying their efforts to reduce CO_2 emissions, aligning with their climate targets.

Studies support this contention. For the PRC, Mao et al. (2023) offer compelling evidence in favor of extending the APEC environmental goods list based on the benefits of market-scale expansion, diversification opportunities, increased sophistication, and value-added of traded goods. To capitalize on the benefits of emerging environmentally friendly goods, technologies, and innovations, APEC is contemplating the addition of new products to the environmental goods list, furthering its commitment to addressing environmental challenges and reinforcing environmental protection and resource management (APEC 2021).

---

[21]   In addition, three WTO trade and environment plurilateral initiatives, TESSD, DPP, and FFSR, issued MC13 statements.
[22]   See WTO (2024) and list in References the flwg details: World Trade Organization (WTO). 2024. Ministerial Declaration on the Contribution of the Multilateral Trading System to Tackle Environmental Challenges. directdoc.aspx (wto.org).
[23]   See Table A2 and Table A3 in Appendix 1 for a range of contending lists covering goods and services identified as "environmental."

Progress on liberalizing trade in environmental goods and services has been modest and mixed. That first point can be appreciated from the data in Figure 5.1, which show that as of 2018–2021 the average tariffs that Asia and Pacific economies apply on imports of a wide range of environmental goods were marginally lower when compared to the rates in 2007–2010. Some of these tariffs were reduced more substantially than others, as in the case of environmentally preferable products, while other goods saw smaller cuts (e.g., those used for waste management). None of these categories of environmental goods benefited from duty-free treatment across-the-board, being generally in the range of 4%–8%.

The data in Figure 5.2 offers a more complex picture for the subregions. Average tariffs on EG imports from the world are only slightly lower than tariffs on all imports; in the case of South Asia, EGs actually face slightly higher-than-average tariffs. As for intraregional trade, the data also show that, on average, preferences in this sector are modest. The one exception to the general rule is the Advanced Asian countries, whose imports of EGs from the region are subject to tariffs only a fraction as high as those imposed on imports from the world; the margin of preference is nonetheless diluted by the fact that Advanced Asian tariffs on these goods—and on all others—tend to be relatively low. Preferences offered by other subregions to Asia and Pacific partners are also notable in the cases of Central Asia and Southeast Asia, but narrower in others.

Figure 5.1: Simple Average Applied Tariffs on Imports of Environmental Goods into Asia and the Pacific from the World, 2007–2010 and 2018–2021

(4-year averages)

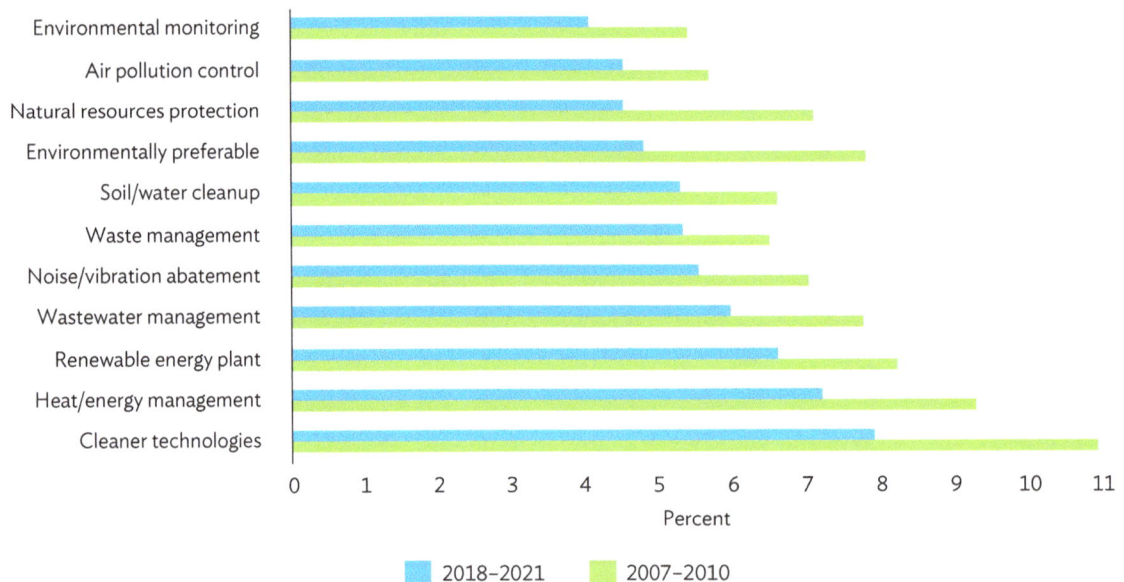

Source: Asian Development Bank calculations using data from World Integrated Trade Solutions (WITS) database. https://wits.worldbank.org/ (accessed 31 March 2024).

Figure 5.2: Tariffs on Environmental Goods by Asian Subregions, 2008–2021
(simple average applied tariffs, %)

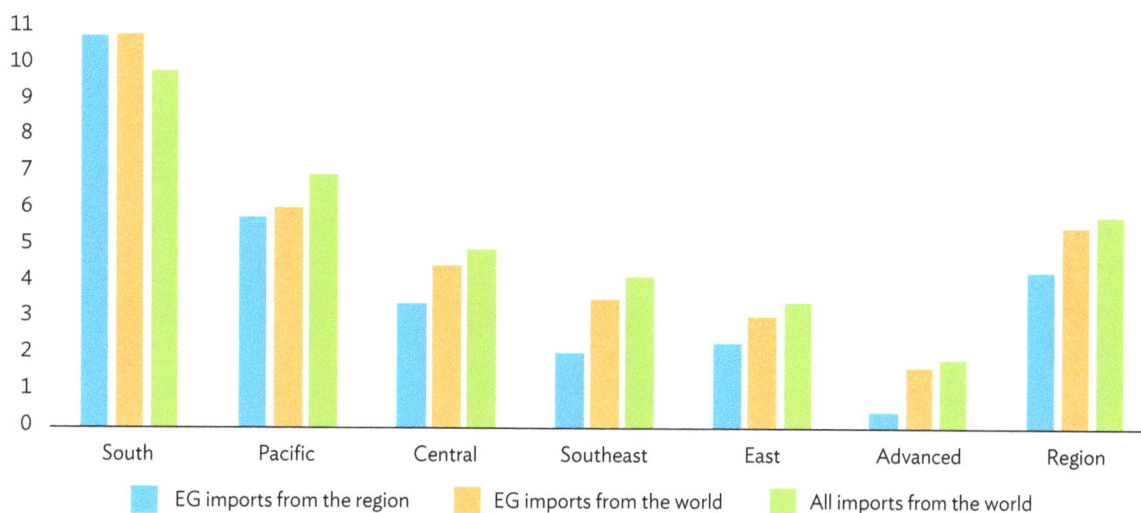

EG = environmental good, OECD = Organisation for Economic Co-operation and Development.
Note: Average applied tariff rates are calculated for 248 environment goods in the OECD list.
Source: Asian Development Bank calculations using data from World Integrated Trade Solutions. WITS Database. https://wits.worldbank.org/ (accessed 31 March 2024).

Trade in environmental services has been given lesser attention compared to trade in goods (Zhuawu and Powell 2022; IISD 2020). At the multilateral level, a counterpart agreement to the WTO Environmental Goods Agreement for services is yet to be realized. Measuring trade in environmental services is challenging, as many environmental services are closely linked with environmental goods and the provision of these services often relies on those related goods (Sauvage 2014).

The lack of shared information on services trade and the difficulty in collecting services data also hinder trade negotiations on environmental services. The Provisional Central Product Classification (CPC) nomenclature defines "core" environment services to include the following: sewage services (CPC 94010); refuse disposal services (CPC 94020); sanitation and similar services (CPC 94030); cleaning services of exhaust gases (CPC 94040); noise abatement services (CPC 94050); nature and landscape protection services (CPC 94060); and other environmental protection services, not elsewhere classified (CPC 94090).

The Regional Comprehensive Economic Partnership Agreement (RCEP), which entered into force in 2022, is considered the largest free trade agreement in the world in terms of output. It builds upon existing agreements between the Association of Southeast Asian Nations (ASEAN) and five of its dialogue partners: Australia, Japan, New Zealand, the PRC, and the Republic of Korea. Compared to ASEAN+1 free trade agreements (FTAs), new disciplines such as competition, intellectual property rights, electronic commerce, and government procurement were also introduced under RCEP. Some observers consider these disciplines modest by comparison to another megaregional agreement, the Comprehensive and Progressive Agreement for Trans-Pacific Partnership (CPTPP) that entered into force in 2018. The scope of CPTPP is broader, including chapters on new trade-related issues such as the environment, state-owned enterprises, labor, business facilitation, and transparency and anti-corruption, among others.[24]

The data in Table 5.1 offer some perspective on RCEP liberalization, based on a method[25] developed by ADB and the Economic Research Institute for ASEAN and East Asia (ERIA) (Crivelli, Marand, and Pascua 2022). The analysis employs that method to quantify the depth of RCEP environment services trade liberalization commitments (CPC 940xx). On the average, environment services

Table 5.1: RCEP Liberalization Rates for Environmental and Other Services

	Mode 1 Cross-Border Supply		Mode 2 Consumption Abroad		Mode 3 Commercial Presence		Mode 4 Movement of Natural Persons	
	All Sectors	Envi Only	All Sectors	Envi Only	All Sectors	Envi Only	All Sectors	Envi Only
Australia	86.0	100.0	99.7	100.0	48.9	74.7	70.4	72.6
Brunei Darussalam	48.8	66.7	100.0	100.0	51.0	95.6	4.3	66.0
People's Republic of China	28.9	38.9	68.4	77.8	49.8	23.7	24.2	20.5
Indonesia	82.9	88.9	92.0	100.0	50.7	39.3	41.3	60.5
Japan	75.9	100.0	98.2	100.0	50.1	100.0	95.4	99.0
Cambodia	37.8	77.8	58.8	77.8	19.9	24.9	18.6	25.7
Republic of Korea	20.4	66.7	61.5	88.9	54.5	86.7	48.9	80.3
Lao People's Democratic Republic	25.5	0.0	49.8	66.7	30.2	17.8	16.6	22.0
Myanmar	51.5	55.6	52.3	55.6	39.9	17.8	4.7	0.0
Malaysia	87.4	33.3	98.7	61.1	43.3	89.6	58.1	55.4
New Zealand	36.0	38.9	40.6	38.9	35.9	20.7	43.6	46.2
Philippines	0.0	0.0	0.0	0.0	12.6	11.9	15.8	14.7
Singapore	63.0	55.6	93.2	100.0	39.5	95.6	48.0	62.3
Thailand	15.4	33.3	63.8	77.8	22.4	20.7	22.2	25.7
Viet Nam	32.6	38.9	74.1	44.4	64.4	48.1	1.0	0.0
Average	46.1	53.0	70.1	72.6	40.9	51.1	34.2	43.4

GATS = General Agreement on Trade in Services, RCEP = Regional Comprehensive Economic Partnership.
Notes: Environmental Services refer to RCEP committed subsectors under (CPC 940xx). Analysis was done at the 4-digit CPC level.
Green refers to economies that used the negative list approach. Blue refers to least developed economies. Yellow cell refers to the higher rate between all sectors and environmental sectors. The use of both positive list and negative list approaches by the RCEP member countries is reflected in the methodology. Uncommitted services subsectors under a positive list approach are assumed to be restricted. Under a negative list approach, the default assumption is that the subsector is open.
Sources: Authors' calculations based on the Asian Development Bank–Economic Research Institute for ASEAN and East Asia RCEP Services Commitments Database. Liberalization rates for all sectors are from the ADB brief prepared by Crivelli, Marand, and Pascua (2022).

---

[24]   ADB provided a preliminary analysis of the RCEP legal text, comparing it with the CPTPP. For more information, see ADB (2022e).
[25]   Further details on the ADB and ERIA methodology can be made available upon request.

under the RCEP are liberalized. However, disparities in the extent of liberalization are observed across member economies and modes of supply. Some of the more notable observations to be made from the data are as follows:

- Australia, Brunei Darussalam, Cambodia, Japan, and the Republic of Korea have higher liberalization rates in environmental services compared to all services sectors for all modes of supply.

- Consumption abroad has the highest degree of commitment, with a 72.6% average liberalization rate in the region.

- Cross-border supply follows with an average of 53.1% and commercial presence with 51.1%; movement of natural persons shows the lowest degree of commitments (43.4%).

- Australia and Japan offered full liberalization of environment services delivered through cross-border supply, while the Lao People's Democratic Republic (Lao PDR) and the Philippines are the least liberalized.

- More economies committed to full liberalization under Consumption Abroad (Mode 2), which includes Australia, Brunei Darussalam, Indonesia, Japan, and Singapore.

- Compared to all services sector commitments, environment services liberalization rates are lower for Malaysia, New Zealand, and Viet Nam, while the Philippines is the most restrictive;

- Delivery through Movement of Natural Persons (Mode 4) is the least restricted for environment services, and most RCEP economies offered more liberalized Mode 4 commitments for environment services compared to all sectors.

- Japan has the most liberalized Mode 4 commitments, while Myanmar and Viet Nam registered restrictions for all contractual services, business visitors, and independent professional movements.

- The highest liberalization rate for Commercial Presence (Mode 3) is in Japan, which committed to full liberalization, followed by Brunei Darussalam, Singapore, Malaysia, the Republic of Korea, and Australia.[26]

The disparity of liberalization rates among RCEP economies under Mode 3 is especially significant, given the importance of commercial presence as a means of delivering services. Additionally, entry of qualified foreign service providers can facilitate the transfer of greener, cheaper, and more advanced equipment and climate-friendly technologies. An Organisation for Economic Co-operation and Development (OECD) (2017) study reported that restrictions on commercial presence are more

---

[26] All of these economies adopted a negative list approach to services liberalization where they provide a list of "non-conforming measures" containing only the limitations and restrictions for specific services sectors and subsectors. By default, sectors not included in this list are by default presumed to be open to foreign suppliers unless otherwise stated (Crivelli, Marand, and Pascua 2022; UNCTAD 2006).

prevalent on broader environmentally related services such as engineering and construction services, and trade restrictions on environmentally related services negatively impacts the supply of core environmental services.

Going beyond core environmental services, recent initiatives such as the Green Economy Agreement (GEA) and APEC's EGS reference list further identify environmentally related services sectors that are incidental to the conduct of environmentally sustainable activities (Annex Table A4). In 2021, APEC endorsed its nonbinding and non-exhaustive Reference List of Environment and Environmentally-Related Services developed using the following criteria: (1) directly relate to environmental conditions; and (2) directly contribute to the design, construction, and operation of facilities or equipment determined to improve environmental conditions (APEC 2021).

Singapore and Australia signed the GEA in 2022, combining trade, economic, and climate objectives. It covers seven key areas of collaboration: trade and investment; standards and conformance; green and transition finance; carbon markets; clean energy, decarbonization, and technology; skills and capabilities; and engagements and partnerships (Government of Singapore 2022). The agreement's environmental services list goes beyond core environment services, encompassing services that feature sustainability and circularity elements; these include services used for the design, construction, and operation of facilities intended to protect or improve environmental conditions; services that support financing of projects with clear environmental benefits; services that improve resource efficiency and sustainable waste management; and services related to the manufacturing, sale, delivery and installation of the environmental goods (Singapore-Australia Green Economy Agreement Annex B 1.2). This innovative agreement is being promoted as a model in support of positive environmental outcome.

Environmental Provisions in PTAs and Their Impact on GVCs and Emissions

Given the challenges in multilateral trade liberalization, bilateral and plurilateral trade agreements have become the main means of liberalizing trade over the past 3 decades. The number of trade agreements have thus expanded rapidly (Figure 5.3). In addition to the rising number of trade agreements, there has also been a widening in the breadth of those agreements, with provisions covering an increasing number of border and behind-the-border issues (Mattoo, Rocha, and Ruta 2020). Using the set of 18 core PTA provisions identified by Hofmann, Osnago, and Ruta (2017), for example, while trade agreements in 1991 covered about 8.5 provisions (48%), on average, that number rose to close to 12 (67%) by 2015 (Figure 5.3).

A further notable trend is that the share of agreements including environmental provisions increased from around 28% in 1991 to 44% in 2022 (Moïsé and Rubínová 2021), suggesting that trade agreements are increasingly used to address environmental concerns between trade partners (Figure 5.3). Back in 2012, for example, APEC members agreed to reduce applied tariff rates on a set of 54 environmental goods to 5% or less by 2020.

Figure 5.3: Number and Breadth of Preferential Trade Agreements

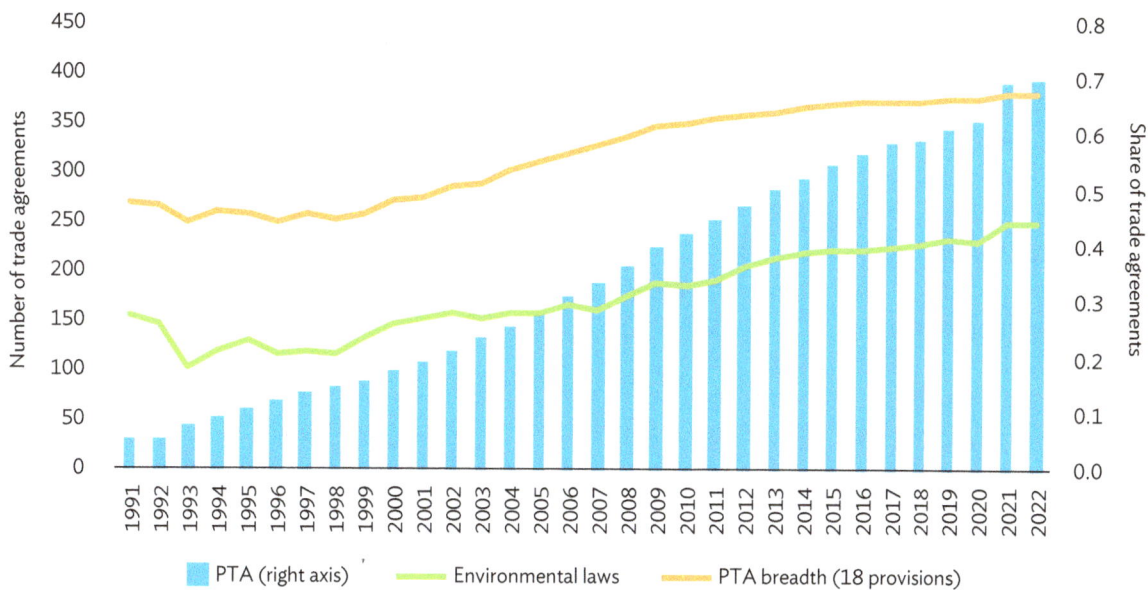

PTA = preferential trade agreement.
Note: The database includes information on 279 PTAs signed by 189 economies during 1958–2022, which includes all PTAs in force and notified to the World Trade Organization.
Source: Elaborated by the authors based on Hofmann, Osnago, and Ruta (2017) and World Bank. Deep Trade Agreements (DTAs): Data, Analysis and Toolkits. https://datatopics.worldbank.org/dta/table.html.

A global monitoring conducted by the OECD observes an increasing number of preferential trade agreements (PTAs) that include environmental provisions over time. However, most of these provisions (about 80%) sought to carve out or identify exceptions for environmental objectives among parties. Around 40% of all agreements made references to specific environmental issues, most notably on biodiversity, circular economy, ocean, land, and energy, among others (OECD 2023).

Environmental provisions can serve many purposes, encouraging trade in clean technologies and raising barriers to trade in dirty goods (Brandi et al. 2020). Beyond the environment, other provisions focused on technology allow PTAs to support the greening of trade and production. Trade agreements increasingly include provisions on the intention to transfer technology, technical cooperation, and research and development (R&D) and innovation. These cover various activities including participation in framework programs on innovation, the promotion of technology transfer and dissemination of new technologies, shared research projects, exchange of researchers, and collaboration on R&D projects (Martinez-Zarzoso and Chelala 2021). In some cases, these provisions have a specific focus on sectors and activities, with the agreement between the European Union and the Caribbean Community (CARICOM), for example, referring to information and communication technology and renewable energy. More controversially, trade agreements increasingly include provisions on intellectual property rights (IPRs) that often go beyond the minimum standards of protection associated with the agreement on Trade-Related Aspects of Intellectual Property Rights. While such provisions can serve the needs of developing economies and be a source of technology diffusion, there are also concerns that these provisions can work against the needs of developing economies. Strong IPRs can create market power, limiting the exports of innovative firms from developed to developing economies. Concerns also arise as to the extent to which strong IPRs limit the adaptive innovation that many currently developed economies have relied on for their development, as well as the risks to the protection of the rights to traditional knowledge in developing economies.

Many agreements include IPR provisions, meaning that this area offers greater scope for the inclusion of climate-friendly provisions in trade pacts. Depending on how they are written, they could support the transfer of green technologies across borders, build up the capabilities of policymakers and labor in developing economies to adopt and adapt green technologies, and help to develop a culture of green innovation. Through trade assistance and capacity building, AfT can further support capabilities to negotiate and implement broader, deeper, and pro-development trade agreements.

Trade is increasingly driven by global value chains (GVCs), splitting up activities so that production is undertaken in different economies. The rise of GVCs has been driven by several factors, including improvements in information and communication technology that facilitate production across geographically distant locations. Reductions in transport costs drive the increase of production within GVCs, with both natural and policy-related trade costs declining in recent decades. PTAs have been shown to enhance GVC trade (Delera and Foster-McGregor 2020), and to create opportunities for developing economies to achieve easier industrialization (Baldwin 2011), gain access to advanced knowledge and technologies, and integrate more easily into the global economy. While the efficiency benefits of GVCs are clear, there are nonetheless concerns that they may generate more GHGs (ADB 2024). Those concerns, in turn, create a motivation for developed countries to use trade policy as a means of mitigating climate change and encouraging a shift to green production.

There are quantitative and qualitative reasons why a trade agreement's environmental provisions might reduce emissions. The first quantitative explanation is that such provisions could raise trade costs between the partners, thus reducing actual commerce. The second qualitative explanation is that environmental provisions could encourage partners to restructure the composition of their trade, changing either the product mix themselves or adopting technological improvements for existing products, which in either case could move those partners toward lower-emission production and commerce.

Figure 5.4 illustrates the results of an estimation of the effect that trade agreements have on the value-added traded between partners in GVCs. Based on structural gravity models, the analysis reveals that the presence of a trade agreement is associated with an increase in GVC trade of around 5.5%; about that same effect is achieved with a shift from no PTA to the broadest trade agreement. An additional PTA provision is thus associated with a 0.3% increase in GVC trade between trade agreement partners. Estimating the model for the trade of exporters by income level reveals substantial differences. The estimates suggest that the presence of a PTA is associated with an increase in GVC exports of around 8.8% for low-income exporters, 7.9% for lower-middle-income exporters, 6.5% for upper-middle-income exporters, and just 2.1% for high-income exporters. A shift from no PTA to the broadest trade agreement is estimated to have even larger effects for low-income exporters, with GVC exports estimated to increase by around 20%. This contrasts with estimated increases of 10.2% in lower-middle-income exporters, 4.7% in upper-middle-income exporters, and 1.4% in high-income exporters.

Figure 5.4: Estimated Impact of PTA Presence and Breadth on GVC Exports, All Economies and Exporters by Income Levels
(%)

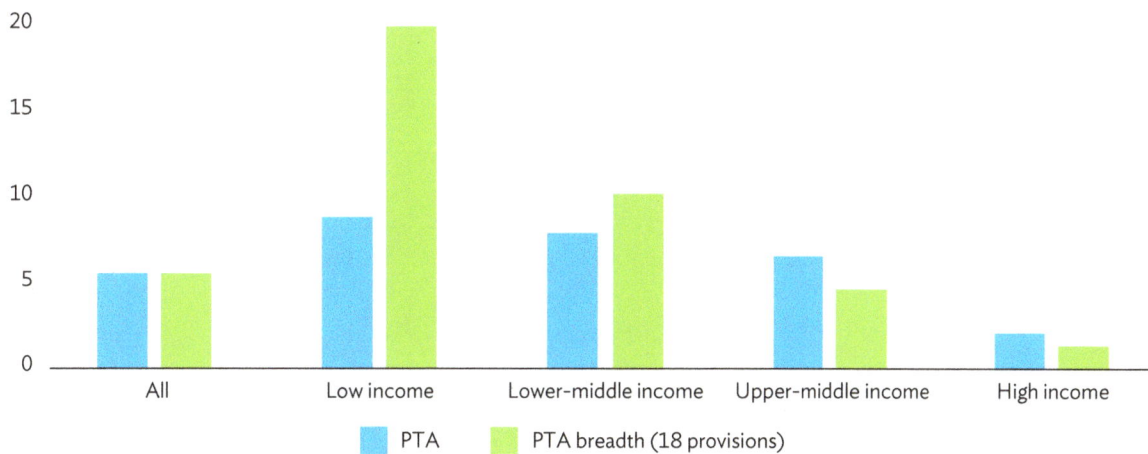

GVC = global value chain, PTA = preferential trade agreement.
Note: The figure reports the estimated coefficient on PTA variables from a structural gravity model of the log of bilateral exports of value-added embodied in GVC trade. The measure of value-added in GVC exports is calculated using the method of Wang et al. (2017) and includes both simple and complex GVC activities. In addition to the PTA variables, the model includes country-pair, exporter-time, and importer-time fixed effects. Data on income status is from the World Bank and refers to the exporting economy.
Source: Asian Development Bank calculations using data from Eora Global Supply Chain Database. https://worldmrio.com/eora26/ (accessed 30 November 2023); Hofmann, Osnago, and Ruta (2017).

The higher levels of trade between trade partners should, all else equal, be associated with higher emissions embodied in trade between trade partners in trade agreements. This is confirmed by Figure 5.5. Estimating similar structural gravity models for the emissions embodied in GVC exports suggests that the presence of a trade agreement increases emissions embodied in trade between trade partners by 6.2%, slightly higher than the trade effect. Once again, the effect is larger for low-income exporters (12.4%) than for lower-middle (12.0%), upper-middle (6.0%), and high-income (2.4%) exporters. Results on the breadth of PTAs also result in larger effects for low-income exporters relative to others. While the effect of moving from no PTA to the broadest trade agreement is estimated at 5.2% for all economies, when considering low-income economies as exporter the effect is estimated at 25.7%. This is substantially larger than the estimates for lower-middle (15.3%), upper-middle (3.9%), and high-income (1.5%) economies.

The results on the effects of PTAs raise the question of whether environmental provisions can ameliorate the emissions effects of trade agreements, while maintaining the benefits of trade agreements in terms of increased exports. Based on a structural gravity model to estimate the relationship between the presence of an environmental provision in trade agreements and its effect on emissions embodied in GVC exports, the data suggest that such a provision is associated with reduced embodied emissions trade by around 4.1% (Figure 5.6). When considering low-income exporters, the estimated effect of an environmental provision is to reduce embodied emissions by 16.3%, with smaller reductions in lower-middle (5.0%) and upper-middle (10.7%) income exporters, and an insignificant increase of 0.4% in high-income exporters.

Figure 5.5: Estimated Impact of PTA Presence and Breadth on Emissions Embodied in GVC Exports, All Economies and Exporters by Income Levels
(%)

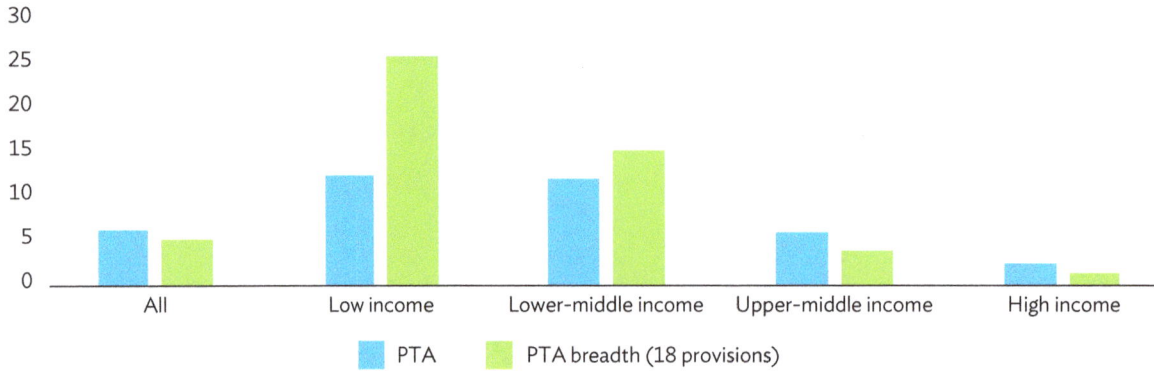

GVC = global value chain, PTA = preferential trade agreement.
Notes: The figure reports the estimated coefficient on PTA variables from a structural gravity model of the log of the bilateral export of carbon dioxide (CO_2) emissions embodied in GVC exports. The measure of emissions embodied in GVC exports is calculated using the method of Wang et al. (2017), replacing the ratio of value-added to gross output with the ratio of CO_2 emissions to gross output in the construction of the measures. In addition to the PTA variables, the model includes country-pair, exporter-time, and importer-time fixed effects. Data on income status is from the World Bank and refers to the exporting economy.
Source: Asian Development Bank calculations using data from Eora Global Supply Chain Database at https://worldmrio.com/eora26/ (accessed 30 November 2023); Hofmann, Osnago, and Ruta (2017).

Figure 5.6: Estimated Impact of PTA Environmental Provisions on GVC Exports and Emissions Embodied in GVC Exports, All Economies and Exporters by Income Levels
(%)

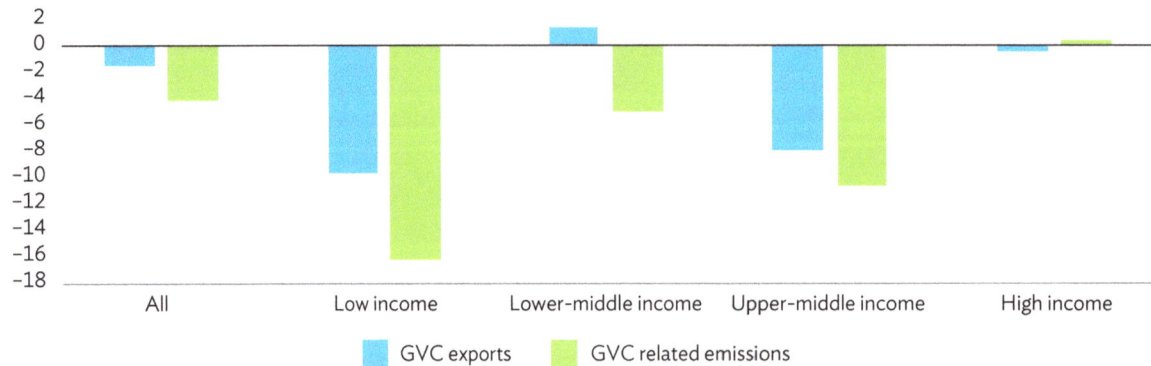

CO_2 = carbon dioxide, GVC = global value chain, PTA = preferential trade agreement.
Notes: The figure reports the estimated coefficient on PTA variables from a structural gravity model of the log of either bilateral exports of value-added embodied in GVC trade or bilateral exports of CO_2 emissions embodied in GVC exports. These indicators are constructed using the method of Wang et al. (2017) and includes both simple and complex GVC activities. The model includes country-pair, exporter-time, and importer-time fixed effects. In addition to the environmental provision variable, a PTA breadth variable is also included such that results on the environmental provisions variables should be interpreted as being conditional on a given level of PTA breadth. Data on income status is from the World Bank and refers to the exporting economy.
Source: Asian Development Bank calculations using data from Eora Global Supply Chain Database at https://worldmrio.com/eora26/ (accessed 30 November 2023); Hofmann, Osnago, and Ruta (2017).

The effect of environmental provisions on GVC exports is also observed to be negative, with the presence of such a provision reducing GVC exports by 1.5%. That this reduction is smaller than the reduction in the emissions embodied in GVC exports indicates that environmental provisions can reduce the emissions effect of trade agreements without removing all the benefits of trade agreements on GVC exports. The reduction in GVC exports being smaller than the reduction in emissions suggests that environmental provisions help reduce emissions intensity of GVC exports by either shifting trade within trade agreements toward cleaner products or by encouraging the adoption of cleaner production techniques for existing products. This is especially true for low-income economies. While the estimated reduction in embodied emissions due to the presence of an environmental provision is 16.3%, the associated reduction in GVC exports is 9.7%. This is also true for lower-middle and upper-middle-income exporters, albeit to a lesser extent:

- For upper-middle-income exporters the 8% reduction in GVC exports is lower than the 10.7% reduction in embodied emissions.

- For both lower-middle and high-income countries there is no significant relationship between environmental provisions and GVC exports.

- For low-income economies, benefits are likely to be stronger if environmental provisions are linked to other provisions in trade agreements, such as those related to technology transfer, as well as economic and technical cooperation.

Considering a graduated implementation of environmental provisions, allowing developing countries more time to adjust to new standards may also help mitigate immediate negative impacts on trade while still moving toward greener production practices. Ensuring an inclusive stakeholder engagement, including environmental nongovernment organizations and industry representatives, in the negotiation of environmental provisions should be prioritized to make these provisions practical, achievable, and beneficial across different sectors.

Given the important role that environmental provisions in trade agreements can play in reducing emissions, side payments (e.g., higher aid flows) may encourage developing economies to sign trade agreements that incorporate environmental provisions (Brandi, Morin, and Stender 2022). These side payments could be further targeted at initiatives for green production in developing economies, allowing them to serve a dual role in enhancing regulatory and legal standards on climate change through the adoption of environmental provisions and enhancing the effects of such provisions through improvements in emissions efficiency.

Chapter 6

Border Carbon Adjustments and Other Trade-Related Climate Measures

Introduction: Pollution Havens and Carbon Leakage

Carbon pricing is increasingly being used to address climate change. Carbon pricing takes two forms: either a carbon tax or an emissions trading scheme (ETS), (also often called a cap and trade system). In recent years, several jurisdictions have implemented policies to create a carbon price through carbon taxes or ETS, with the World Bank (2022) identifying around 70 carbon-pricing initiatives in 39 national jurisdictions. Among the drawbacks of current efforts are that they tend to cover relatively narrow jurisdictions (e.g., cities, states, individual countries), as well as a limited number of products (meaning that they also cover a limited amount of carbon emissions), and the prices of carbon tend to be too low within these schemes to have a significant impact on global emissions. The major exception is the European Union's (EU) ETS, which covers all EU countries (plus others that joined the ETS or are linked to it) and for which the price of carbon has recently been in the range necessary to have an impact on global emissions (i.e., between $60 and $100 per metric ton of CO_2).

To address some of the limitations of current carbon pricing mechanisms, Border Carbon Adjustments (BCAs) have been proposed as a complementary policy tool. Carbon leakage, a significant challenge in global efforts to combat climate change, occurs when production in a country implementing a climate policy is either moved abroad to economies with few or no climate standards, or when goods that might otherwise have been sourced locally will be imported from such economies. For example, this may mean relocating steel production to countries not subject to carbon pricing or importing steel from these countries instead of buying from local producers that are subject to a carbon price, undermining the effectiveness of carbon pricing. BCAs aim to ensure that foreign producers face the same effective carbon price in their export markets as domestic firms, thereby reducing the risk of carbon leakage. Additionally, BCAs can address the broader issue of environmental regulation within global value chains (GVCs), which are often more difficult to regulate due to their international nature (Jakob 2021a). This approach can also mitigate the pollution haven hypothesis, where environmentally harmful production stages are shifted from developed countries with strict regulations to developing countries with less stringent ones. By applying fees on imported goods based on their emissions content, countries with domestic carbon pricing initiatives align the price that an importer pays with the domestic carbon price. In doing so, the policy is intended to remove the incentive for shifting production to regions with a lower price, thus reducing carbon leakage (Bellora and Fontagné 2023; Böhringer, Balistreri, and Rutherford 2012; Branger and Quirion 2014).

How great a problem is carbon leakage? Empirical assessments find that little has occurred to date (Koch and Basse Mama 2019), which can be explained by the fact that energy costs in most industries account only for a small fraction of total production costs. For instance, one study demonstrates that on average a 10% increase in the energy price gap between two countries results in only a 0.2% increase in bilateral imports (Sato and Dechezleprêtre 2015). Nevertheless, a few individual sectors have probably already been subject to carbon leakage. A meta-analysis on model studies by Branger and Quirion (2014) projects leakage rates of 5%–25% (with a mean of 14%). More important is the prospect of future carbon leakage if some countries ramp up climate policies while others lag behind.

BCAs in Theory: The Economics of Carbon Leakage and Carbon Pricing

Böhringer et al. (2022) argue that the extent of the carbon leakage will depend on the extent of differences in emissions-intensity between firms in the jurisdiction with carbon pricing and the trade partners to which production shifts, as well as the exposure to trade of the products subject to carbon pricing. While evidence of significant carbon leakage is currently limited (European Parliament 2020; Verde 2020; Cherniwchan and Taylor 2022), there are concerns that the extent of such leakage may increase as the price of carbon inevitably increases in jurisdictions that are seeking to mitigate climate change through carbon pricing, with current prices incompatible with longer term decarbonization goals (Grubb et al. 2022).

A global uniform carbon price would be economically efficient and in parallel avoid carbon leakage (Böhringer et al. 2022; Carbon Pricing Leadership Coalition 2017; Cramton et al. 2017). Relocation of emissions-intensive production would then occur only to the extent that it is economically desirable to shift production to more climate-friendly locations, for instance, those with abundant renewable energy supplies. However, global negotiations for a uniform carbon price have halted, resulting in a variety of heterogeneous, unilateral, and uncoordinated climate policies. As an internationally agreed solution through multilateral and plurilateral initiatives remains uncertain and lengthy to develop, divergences in global climate ambition and policy approaches are likely to persist in the medium term, thus requiring near- and medium-term domestic policy action. Multilateral and plurilateral initiatives can support the implementation of BCAs by developing interoperable standards and approaches, for example for embedded emissions and agreed default emissions intensities, enhancing effectiveness and transparency.

The competitiveness impacts of climate policies implemented in Asian countries crucially depend on the costs that climate policies in other countries impose on firms located there, and thus the competitive position of producers in Asia might even improve with climate policy if they either can produce at lower emissions intensity or if other countries have more stringent policies. A BCA may undermine the competitiveness of local companies that depend on imported goods, and the risk is especially high if intermediate and carbon-intensive commodities cannot be substituted. In the case of full border adjustments with export rebates installed for companies producing within a carbon pricing entity, exporters would be compensated for carbon prices already paid once their goods leave for a foreign market where no or less ambitious carbon pricing is applied. To ensure that BCAs are in line with the WTO non-discrimination principles, they must not overcompensate by creating a net advantage for local companies. Similarly, any coverage of such a second step must not exceed the coverage and stringency of domestic regulations. It might be that applying different rates to the same product category because of heterogeneous carbon intensities also results in discriminatory treatments (Böhringer et al. 2022; Zhong and Pei 2024; Mehling et al. 2019; Takeda and Arimura 2024).

Broader legal issues should be considered in the design of climate-related border measures. For example, these measures could potentially contravene the principle of common but differentiated responsibility of the United Nations Framework Convention on Climate Change (UNFCCC), as well as Article 3.5 of that convention, which states that climate change mitigation measures should not serve as a "disguised restriction on international trade" or involve "arbitrary and unjustifiable discrimination." By imposing new tariffs, BCAs may reduce global demand for imported goods, driving down prices and worsening the terms of trade for those exporters covered (Bellora and Fontagné 2023; Böhringer et al. 2010; UNCTAD 2021). Such effects may fall disproportionately on developing economies that are important GVC suppliers of energy-intensive products (Böhringer et al. 2022; Beaufils et al. 2023).

In the context of AfT, it is critical to note that competitiveness will be affected in the absence of climate measures in third-party countries. This is because economies will be heterogeneously impacted by climate change and specifically extreme events such as heatwaves, extreme rainfall, or changes in the monsoon. Specifically for countries with the highest relative projected climate impacts and limited resources to adapt, such as developing Asian economies, a ramp-up of climate measures might be in their own interests, also under consideration of economic competitiveness.

A BCA in Practice: The European Union's CBAM

Moving from theory to practice, the introduction of the EU's Carbon Border Adjustment Mechanism (CBAM) is the first of its kind, but it will surely not be the last. The United Kingdom has announced that it will introduce its own CBAM in 2027,[27] and discussions are also underway in Canada, the United States, and other developed countries. It is therefore of utmost importance to learn from the first CBAM to understand how these mechanisms function in practice, especially for developing and least developed countries that may be disproportionately affected due to higher emissions intensities, weaker institutional quality and capabilities, and an undiversified trade structure.

The main rationale for adopting CBAM is carbon leakage.[28] The danger of such leakage has been a concern in developed countries since the first commitment period of the Kyoto Protocol, which required developed and transition countries to reduce emissions by 5% below 1990 levels in the

---

[27] See https://www.gov.uk/government/consultations/addressing-carbon-leakage-risk-to-support-decarbonisation/outcome/factsheet-uk-carbon-border-adjustment-mechanism.

[28] Carbon Border Adjustment Mechanism: Questions and Answers, Brussels, 28 February 2024, https://taxation-customs.ec.europa.eu/carbon-border-adjustment-mechanism_en (accessed 3 June 2024).

first commitment period (2008–2012) and by 18% in the second period (2013–2020), with no binding targets for developing countries. There was a trend reversal in CO_2 emissions for developed countries in 2008, while unregulated emissions continued to rise for developing countries. The trends are the same whether emissions are measured from the production or the consumption side, the latter referring to the emissions embedded in the consumption of both domestic and imported products.[29]

Such a policy also speaks to an issue of political sustainability: CBAM can lower domestic opposition to carbon-pricing from input producers in the EU by easing concerns over the potential loss of competitiveness and market share from stringent climate policies. What tipped the political balance in favor of the CBAM, after several earlier proposals had been rejected by member states,[30] was the combined effect of the increased target in the Fit for 55 program, frustration with the uneven and insufficient nationally determined contributions (NDCs) in the Paris Agreement, and the quadrupling of the carbon price in the EU ETS in 2021 and 2022. The carbon price in that ETS is currently around €60 per ton of CO_2, or about 10 times the global average. Such a price differential may be difficult for EU industry to absorb through green innovation and cost reductions and may therefore induce some carbon leakage. How much leakage can be expected is debatable, but in the empirical literature the ballpark range is 10%–30%.[31]

The CBAM entered into force on 1 October 2023. It covers cement, iron and steel, aluminum, fertilizers, electricity, and hydrogen production.[32] As summarized in Box 6.1, the CBAM provides for a transition period before the permanent regime enters into effect. In its transition phase, importers of CBAM-covered goods will report emissions embedded in their imports without incurring financial costs. Indirect emissions will be included only after the transition phase, and only for some sectors (fertilizers and cement), with the transition phase offering an opportunity to develop methods for the calculation of indirect emissions. The transition phase will further be used as an opportunity to assess the product scope of CBAM and whether additional products covered by the ETS should fall under CBAM. After the transition phase, EU imports of goods covered by CBAM will need to obtain certificates, which will be priced based on ETS allowances. They will then declare the emissions embedded in their imports and surrender the corresponding number of certificates. This can be reduced if the importer can prove that a carbon price has already been paid on the imports during production. From January 2026, the price of GHG emissions will be the same for domestic and foreign producers in the EU market, but not in the wider global market, where differences will remain until carbon prices converge globally.

---

[29] See Nordström (2023) for data sources and the methodology for calculating the emissions from the consumption side, using global input output models.

[30] The negotiation history from the first "FAIR" proposal in 2007 (Future Allowance Import Requirements) to the CBAM proposal in 2021 is outlined in a report by the National Board of Trade (2023), Sweden, on the WTO consistency of the CBAM proposal.

[31] The literature on carbon leakage is reviewed by Caron (2022), who puts the approximate range of carbon leakage at 10%–30%. Similar results are found by Böhringer, Carbone, and Rutherford (2018) and Verde (2020). However, these estimates are based on the commitments under the Kyoto Protocol and may not be relevant to the current situation.

[32] See Appendix 1 for a more complete description and listing of the affected goods.

Box 6.1: The Carbon Border Adjustment Mechanism's Transitional Rules and the Permanent Regime

During the transition period from 1 October 2023 to 31 December 2025, there will be no charge for reported emissions. The purpose of the 2-year transition period is to allow importers and exporters to adapt to the new system in an orderly manner and to fine-tune administrative procedures.

During the transition period, importers and customs agents acting on behalf of exporters are required to submit quarterly Carbon Border Adjustment Mechanism (CBAM) reports. These reports should be submitted no later than 1 month after the end of the reporting period. As it turned out, this deadline was not feasible for the first reporting period, partly because of technical problems with the electronic reporting platform. According to the *Financial Times* (1 March 2024), citing the German and Swedish environmental protection agencies, only 10%–11% of the expected CBAM reports were received on time. This was not only because of technical glitches, but also because many importers were unaware of the new obligations or had difficulty collecting the data from their overseas supply network.

The European Commission anticipated some initial problems, and the transitional rules provide some flexibility for the first three periods to get the system up and running. First, in addition to the general extension of the first deadline by 1 month due to the technical problems, reporters were allowed to fill in the holes in the first CBAM reports until the end of May 2024. Secondly, reporters who were unable to provide actual emissions data could instead fill in the default values in the regulations, which are based on the "global average" calculated by the Joint Research Centre on data from the largest exporters to the European Union (EU) of CBAM goods.

The real test of the system will come in the fourth reporting period, starting in July 2024, when actual emissions data will have to be reported using the methodology set out in the CBAM Regulation. From then on, late or incomplete CBAM reports can also be penalized by the Commission to put pressure on reporters, with fines ranging from €5 to €50 per tonne of carbon dioxide (CO_2).

Once the permanent system enters into force on 1 January 2026, embedded emissions will be reported annually by 31 May instead of quarterly. The reported emissions must be covered by an equal amount of CBAM allowances purchased in advance from the competent authority in each member state. The price of the emissions is determined by the average weekly auction price of EU emissions trading scheme (ETS) allowances, expressed in €/tonne of CO_2 emitted, currently around €60 per tonne (April 2024). Unlike the cap on EU ETS allowances, there is no cap on the number of CBAM certificates that can be issued.

The requirement to surrender CBAM certificates will apply to all countries except the three members of the European Economic Area (Iceland, Norway, Liechtenstein) that are part of the EU ETS. There's also a special arrangement for Switzerland, whose domestic ETS is linked to the EU ETS. This link means that allowances issued under the Swiss system and those issued under the EU system are mutually recognized, allowing participants to use allowances from either system for compliance.

To avoid double taxation, exporters can provide verified data on the carbon prices they have paid domestically for the units exported to the EU. If the carbon price is equivalent to that in the EU, no carbon certificates need to be surrendered. Deductions should also be made for the proportion of free allowances received by installations in the EU ETS, a legacy of the system's introduction in 2005, which will be phased out by 2030.

Source: : Authors' research.

Trade Exposure to the CBAM

The responsibility for reporting emissions under the CBAM falls on EU importers. They are required to register as CBAM declarants with their respective national authorities, typically the environmental protection agency in each member state. While it might seem unconventional to place this burden on importers when the data originates from overseas producers, the CBAM regulation holds importers accountable for any inaccuracies or omissions (European Commission 2023). This means that in practice importers and exporters must agree on the standards and routines for providing the data and for ensuring its accuracy (e.g., third-party verification). Importers may require independent verification to protect themselves from liability, which may be impractical and too expensive for small exporters and be a viable option only for larger producers. Placing the onus on importers may therefore be a barrier to trade for smaller foreign exporters to the EU. It may also be more costly than a system allowing direct reporting, taking into account the fees charged by the intermediary. At a minimum, we can thus be certain that CBAM will increase compliance costs in some industries by requiring them to keep records and file statements that had not previously been required. In this sense, it is the opposite of what WTO members sought in negotiating the paperwork-reducing terms of the Trade Facilitation Agreement.

Which economies are at greatest risk? The data in Figure 6.1 indicate that they vary greatly in their dependence on emissions-intensive goods, ranging from 4% to 98%, and that dependence tends to be associated with a few industry sectors. There are only six economies in the region for which emissions-intensive goods account for at least two-thirds of their exports, and in each case they are heavily dependent on mineral exports. The association is not absolute, as can be seen from the cases of three economies for which minerals accounted for more than half of total exports but emissions-intensive goods were at or near one-third of total exports (i.e., Armenia, Fiji, and Myanmar). Other industry sectors are only somewhat correlated with levels of dependence on emissions-intensive goods.

The data in Table 6.1 further suggest that the exposure may vary widely across Asia and Pacific economies, depending on the degrees to which (1) CBAM products figure in their exports to the EU, and (2) the EU market predominates in their exports of these goods. For the average economy in the region—a position approximated by the PRC—the CBAM-affected goods constitute about 3%–4% of their exports to the EU, and that market takes roughly 10% of their exports of these goods. These averages hide the outliers, which cover a wide range. At one end of the spectrum, CBAM-related goods account for over half of Armenia's exports to the EU, which takes in more than two-thirds of its exports of these goods; six other economies in the region likewise face above-average exposure to the CBAM. At the other extreme, these goods account for less than 1% of 10 economies' exports to the EU, and that market takes in less than 5% of the exports of such goods from nine economies.

Figure 6.1: Composition of Exports of Emissions-Intensive Goods, 2022

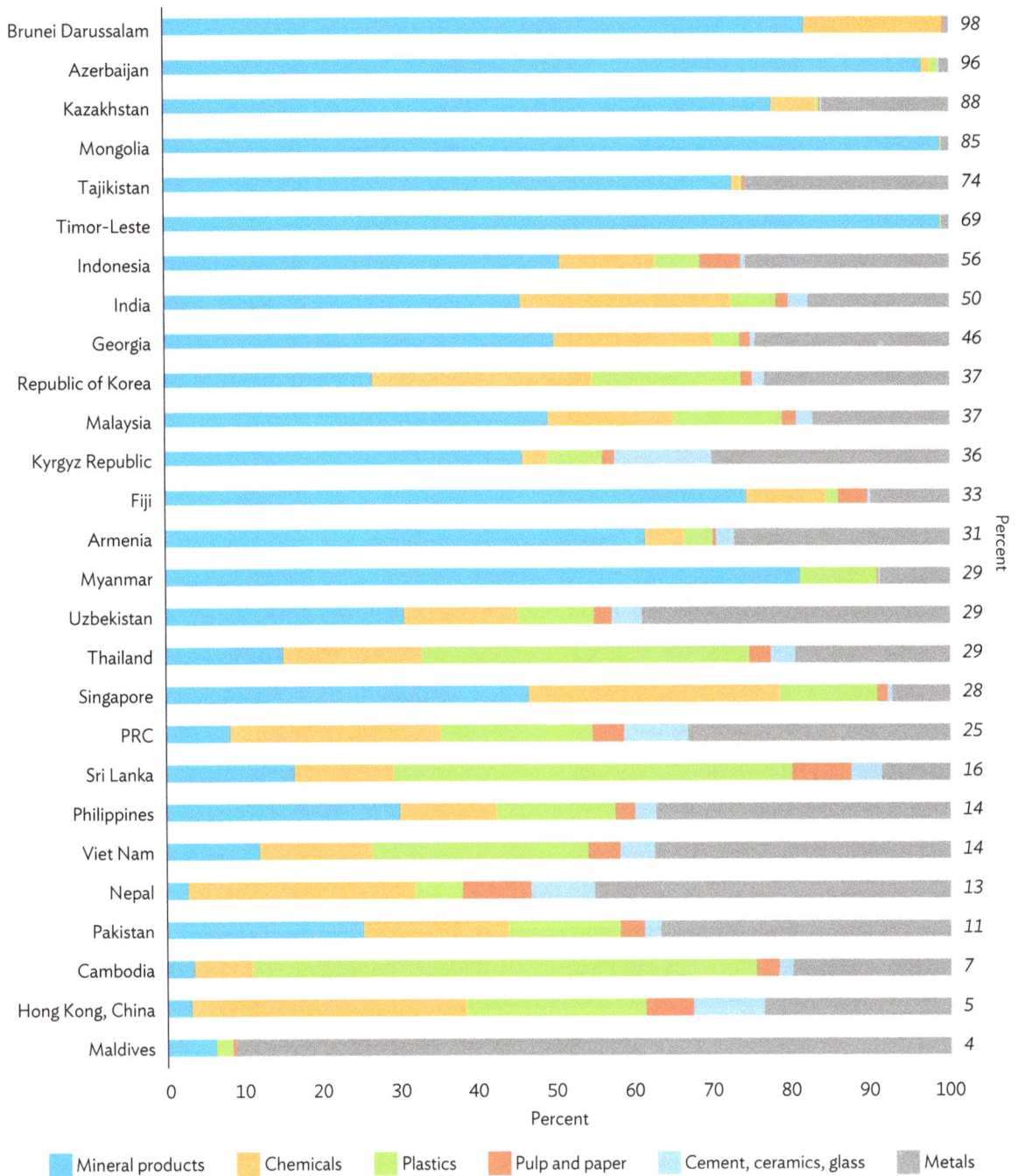

PRC = People's Republic of China.
Note: Share of emissions-intensive goods in total 2022 exports shown in *italics*.
Source: Authors' depiction based on data from COMTRADE (2024).

Table 6.1: Vulnerability of Asia and Pacific Economies to the EU CBAM, 2021–2022

	CBAM Products in Exports to the EU (%)	Share of Total CBAM Product Exports Going to the EU (%)
Above-Average Exposure		
Armenia	52.1	68.8
India	12.1	25.5
Republic of Korea	7.4	12.3
Uzbekistan	35.2	24.2
Papua New Guinea	6.8	24.2
Tajikistan	3.8	17.5
Viet Nam	6.8	17.5
Approximately Average Exposure		
People's Republic of China	3.0	9.9
Asia and Pacific Average	3.8	10.5
Mixed Exposure		
Azerbaijan	0.8	19.9
Brunei Darussalam	4.5	3.0
Georgia	9.5	8.9
Indonesia	6.4	3.4
Kazakhstan	3.0	13.1
Malaysia	5.2	8.7
Myanmar	35.2	0.2
Tonga	0.8	19.9
Below-Average Exposure		
Australia	1.7	4.3
Bhutan	1.7	4.3
Cambodia	0.3	10.1
Hong Kong, China	0.3	7.4
Japan	2.6	5.0
Kyrgyz Republic	0.8	0.8
Nepal	0.3	0.7
New Zealand	2.6	7.2
Pakistan	0.2	3.1
Philippines	0.3	3.4
Singapore	0.7	6.1
Sri Lanka	0.2	9.2
Thailand	1.9	5.2

CBAM = Carbon Border Adjustment Mechanism, EU = European Union.
Notes: Above-Average Exposure = Values on both measures were equal to or above the average for the region. Approximately Average Exposure = The People's Republic of China comes within one percentage point for each of the regional averages. Mixed Exposure = Economies for which one measure was below, and one another above, the average for the region. Below-Average Exposure = Economies for which the values on both measures were below the average for the region. Calculations are based on average 2021–2022 exports.
Source: Authors' calculations based on UN COMTRADE.

The Impact of CBAM—A Computable General Equilibrium Model

To estimate more precisely the actual or potential impact of the CBAM on specific economies and sectors, two approaches can be adopted. One is an ex post approach based on a regression that looks retrospectively at actual imports. Using quarterly data from 2017 to 2023, Nordström (2024) finds that large import flows from countries with relatively low emissions seem to be preferred by EU importers since the third quarter of 2023. This suggests that importers have already started adjusting to CBAM during its first phase by internalizing the administrative fixed costs associated with each CBAM report, the taxes on unreported actual emissions from July 2024, and future CO_2 levies. However, results should be read with caution as more data and analytical studies will become available in the coming months.

Another approach, as reviewed below, is to devise a model that seeks to forecast imports prospectively. Computable general equilibrium (CGE) models are commonly used to examine the potential consequences of changes to trade and other policies. The models combine economic theory that identifies the structure of an economy and behavioral responses of agents (e.g., firms, households, and governments) with real-world data to model the potential effects of policies on economies. Comparing an initial baseline case with estimated outcomes following some change in policy (in this case CBAM), allows for an ex ante estimate of the effect of policy interventions. Unlike partial equilibrium models, an important advantage of CGE modeling is that it allows for interactions between different sectors, agents, and markets, meaning that effects that work through the reorientation of value chains (among other effects) are also considered. This added complexity makes interpretation of results more challenging, however, with the direct effects of policy interventions potentially being reinforced or counteracted by indirect effects that work through changes in relative prices.

Generally, interventions such as CBAM generate two opposing effects, an income and a substitution effect. Considering the EU ETS, the imposition of the ETS (or an increase in the carbon price) will raise the cost of inputs provided domestically, which can lead to a substitution of production to alternative sources where no carbon pricing is in place. This would be expected to raise emissions, production, and exports in the rest of the world, with the opposite effect in the EU. At the same time, the higher production costs in response to the ETS will lower EU production levels and income, with negative consequences for global demand and for output and exports from the rest of the world. The overall impact of the ETS on global production, emissions, and exports is thus ambiguous.

Additional forces are at play in the case of CBAM: It will increase the price of inputs imported into the EU from third countries, as they are now subject to a carbon price. The extent of this increase depends on the emissions-intensity of the imported products, and whether they are already subject to a domestic carbon price. This would be expected to lead to a substitution of input demand back toward EU producers. With all inputs used in EU production subject to a carbon price, the cost of downstream production in the EU will increase, which can encourage downstream producers to shift production out of the EU. This incentive exists because downstream production is not subject to CBAM, meaning that the emissions embodied in inputs that are embodied in final imported goods are not subject to carbon pricing. Through this effect, production and exports of downstream products may increase in the rest of the world. Income effects also play a role, with the higher EU carbon price reducing output and income levels further, entailing negative consequences for output and exports in all regions. Once again, therefore, the overall impacts of CBAM on emissions, production, and trade are ambiguous.

A CGE model is used to estimate the effect of CBAM on the output and exports of different countries and regions. Specifically, it is assumed that the EU does two things simultaneously: (1) it increases the price of carbon in the EU ETS from €18 per metric ton of CO_2 to €100 per metric ton; and (2) it imposes a CBAM on imported inputs also at the price of €100 per metric ton of CO_2. The overall estimated effects will capture these two dimensions of a higher ETS carbon price and the imposition of a border carbon adjustment.

Figure 6.2 reports the estimated impact of this policy change on output, exports, and exports to the EU for a range of countries and regions. The effects of the extended ETS and CBAM are negative for all countries and regions. Unsurprisingly, the effects are largest for EU countries, which see reductions in GDP of just under 2% and export reductions of around 2.7%. These reflect the strong substitution effects associated with the higher ETS price and income effects due to the higher costs of production in the EU. Effects for extra-European countries are heterogeneous:

- Other Organisation for Economic Co-operation and Development (OECD) Europe also sees relatively strong declines, representing the fact that some are also part of the EU ETS and their strong trade links with the EU.

- Reductions in output of 0.22% and 0.14% are estimated for low-income Southeast Asia and low-income South Asia, respectively, effects that are lower than for other economies in these regions.

- Export reductions of more than 1% are estimated for Other South Asia, West and North Africa, Central and West Asia, Other Europe, Sub-Saharan Africa, Australia, and New Zealand, Latin America, Indonesia, and India.

- Exports to the EU are even more strongly affected in regions that tend to be geographically close, are important suppliers, and are relatively emissions-inefficient, such as West and North Africa, Central and West Asia, Sub-Saharan Africa, and Other Europe.

While the estimated negative output effects of CBAM on most countries and regions is estimated to be muted, the overall impacts on low-income countries could be magnified by their lack of resources and ability to respond to CBAM through domestic carbon pricing or the upgrading of production technologies. Moreover, the effects on these countries could strengthen as the coverage of CBAM is extended and as other countries and regions consider the imposition of similar schemes. There are compelling reasons to support such countries in adapting to CBAM, therefore, including using the substantial CBAM revenue that is expected to be generated (Perdana and Vielle 2022).

Figure 6.2: Estimated Impact of CBAM on Output and Exports by Country and Region
(percentage change relative to baseline)

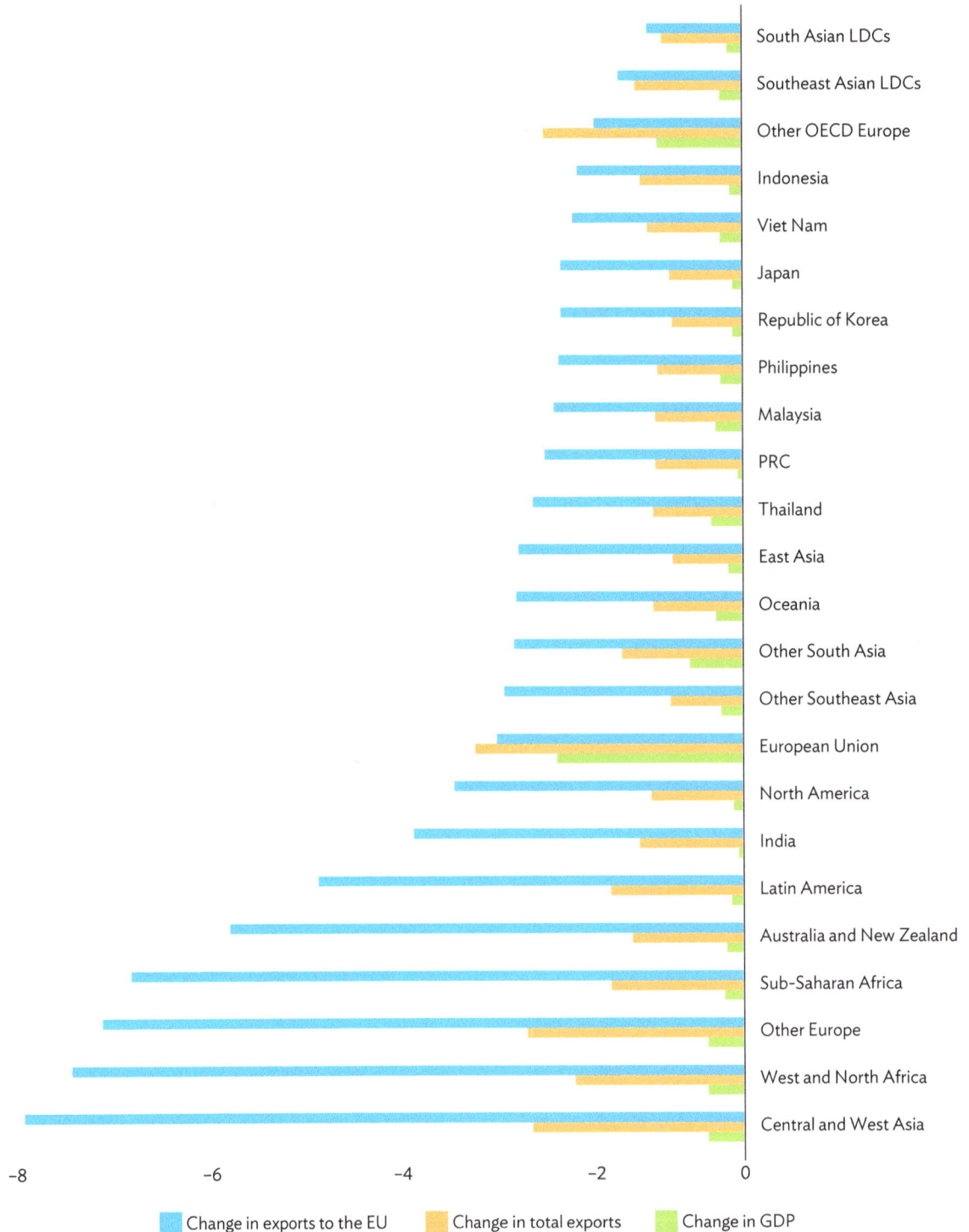

Change in exports to the EU   Change in total exports   Change in GDP

CBAM = Carbon Border Adjustment Mechanism, EU = European Union, GDP = gross domestic product, LDC = least developed country, OECD = Organisation for Economic Co-operation and Development, PRC = People's Republic of China.
Sources: Global Trade Analysis Project 11 (https://www.gtap.agecon.purdue.edu/databases/v11/) and International Energy Agency (https://www.iea.org/data-and-statistics) (both accessed 30 November 2023).

One means of supporting these countries is through encouraging the diffusion and adoption of cleaner technologies that can reduce emissions intensity. This will have the dual benefit of reducing low-income countries' exposure to CBAM tariffs, while also contributing to global cleaning of production. While the cost of such support is difficult to calculate using modeling exercises, it is possible to consider the effects of successful efforts to clean production by considering the impacts on output and exports from a convergence in emissions intensities toward the best performers. The analysis below focuses on the case of Asia and considers two scenarios:

1. Following the extension of the ETS and imposition of CBAM, non-LDC Asian economies see a convergence of 25% in their emissions intensities toward those of the OECD.

2. Following the extension of the ETS and imposition of CBAM, non-LDC Asian economies see a convergence of 25% in their emissions intensities toward those of the OECD, while LDC Asian economies see a convergence of 75% toward intensities in the OECD.

The first scenario is intended to consider a possible response of those countries in Asia that are more able to respond to the incentives that CBAM provides, while the latter is intended to provide some indication of what a successful effort to diffuse green technologies to LDCs in Asia could achieve.

Figure 6.3 presents the results of the model assuming convergence in the emissions intensities of non-LDC Asia. Convergence in emissions intensities toward the OECD average is found to have positive effects on output in most Asian countries and regions. These effects are found to be substantial in India (8.4%), Indonesia (8.4%), Thailand (7.1%), Central and West Asia (6.6%), and the PRC (5.8%). In many cases, these increases in production are also associated with substantial increases in exports, notably in India and Indonesia. The destination of those exports is more varied, however. India is estimated to see large increases in exports to the EU, presumably reflecting its improved competitiveness in inputs that are in demand in the EU. Conversely, Indonesian exports to the EU are estimated to fall despite the large increase in exports generally, likely reflecting improved competitiveness in downstream sectors serving the rest of the world, for example, by increasing downstream leakage from the EU and other regions subject to high CBAM tariffs. These results highlight the positive benefits in terms of output and exports that investments in clean technologies can achieve following the implementation of CBAM. Such improvements can improve global competitiveness by reallocating production to countries with improved emissions intensities.

Introducing emissions intensity convergence in Asian LDCs does not have a major impact on the output or exports of other Asian countries and regions. It does result in substantial changes in output in Asian LDCs, however. Compared to the reductions of 0.22% and 0.14% in output in Southeast Asian and South Asian LDCs in response to the imposition of CBAM, respectively, emissions intensity convergence in these countries is estimated to increase output by 3.9% and 2.0%, respectively. These are also larger than the estimated increases in output for these regions from convergence in emissions for other Asian countries, increases estimated at 0.4% and 0.75% for Southeast Asian and South Asian LDCs, respectively. Emissions intensity convergence more than offsets the reduction in exports that the imposition of CBAM was estimated to have, with exports increasing by 1% and 3% for Southeast Asian and South Asian countries, respectively, relative to the baseline scenario. The observation that exports to the EU are barely changed from the baseline

Figure 6.3: Estimated Impacts of Emissions Convergence in Non-LDC Asia
(percentage change relative to baseline)

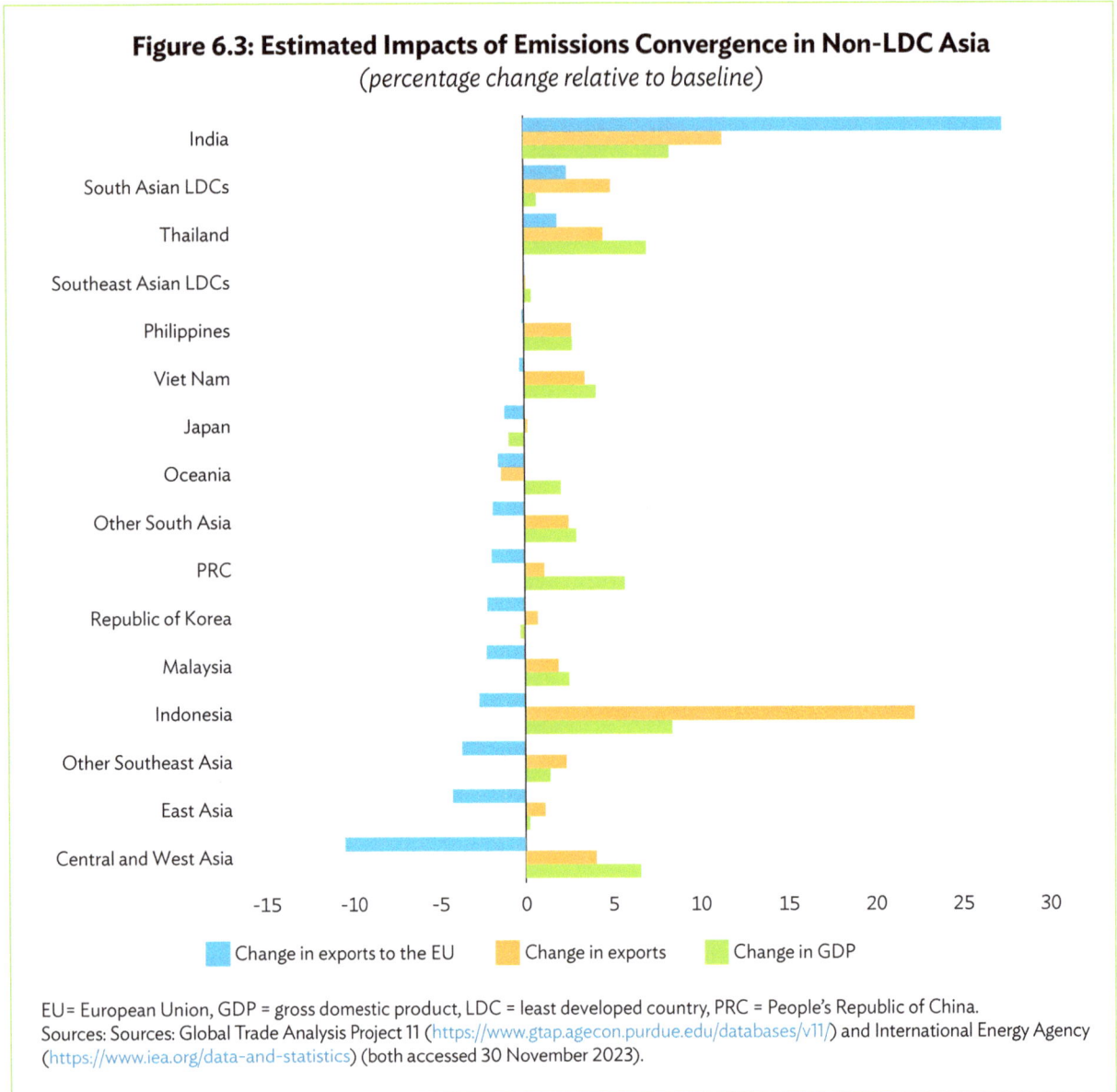

EU= European Union, GDP = gross domestic product, LDC = least developed country, PRC = People's Republic of China.
Sources: Sources: Global Trade Analysis Project 11 (https://www.gtap.agecon.purdue.edu/databases/v11/) and International Energy Agency (https://www.iea.org/data-and-statistics) (both accessed 30 November 2023).

scenario indicates that LDCs are likely to capture some of the downstream leakage that occurs from the EU and from countries subject to stronger CBAM tariffs (i.e., more emissions-intensive) following CBAM's imposition.

Considering the combined effects of CBAM and the different emissions intensity convergence scenarios, Figure 6.4 reports estimated changes in sectoral output for LDCs in Southeast Asia and South Asia. While magnitudes vary across the two regions, the pattern of changes is quite similar. Output is estimated to drop in both sets of countries in ferrous metals, nonferrous metals, and mining, with drops estimated in metals for South Asian LDCs and in gas manufacture and petrochemicals in Southeast Asia. The estimated drops are most substantial in ferrous and nonferrous metals, with the biggest driver of these changes being the imposed improvements in emissions efficiency in non-LDC Asia through convergence in emissions intensity. These improvements are estimated to

**Figure 6.4: Estimated Impacts of CBAM and Emissions Convergence
on Sectoral Output in Asian LDCs**
(percentage change relative to baseline)

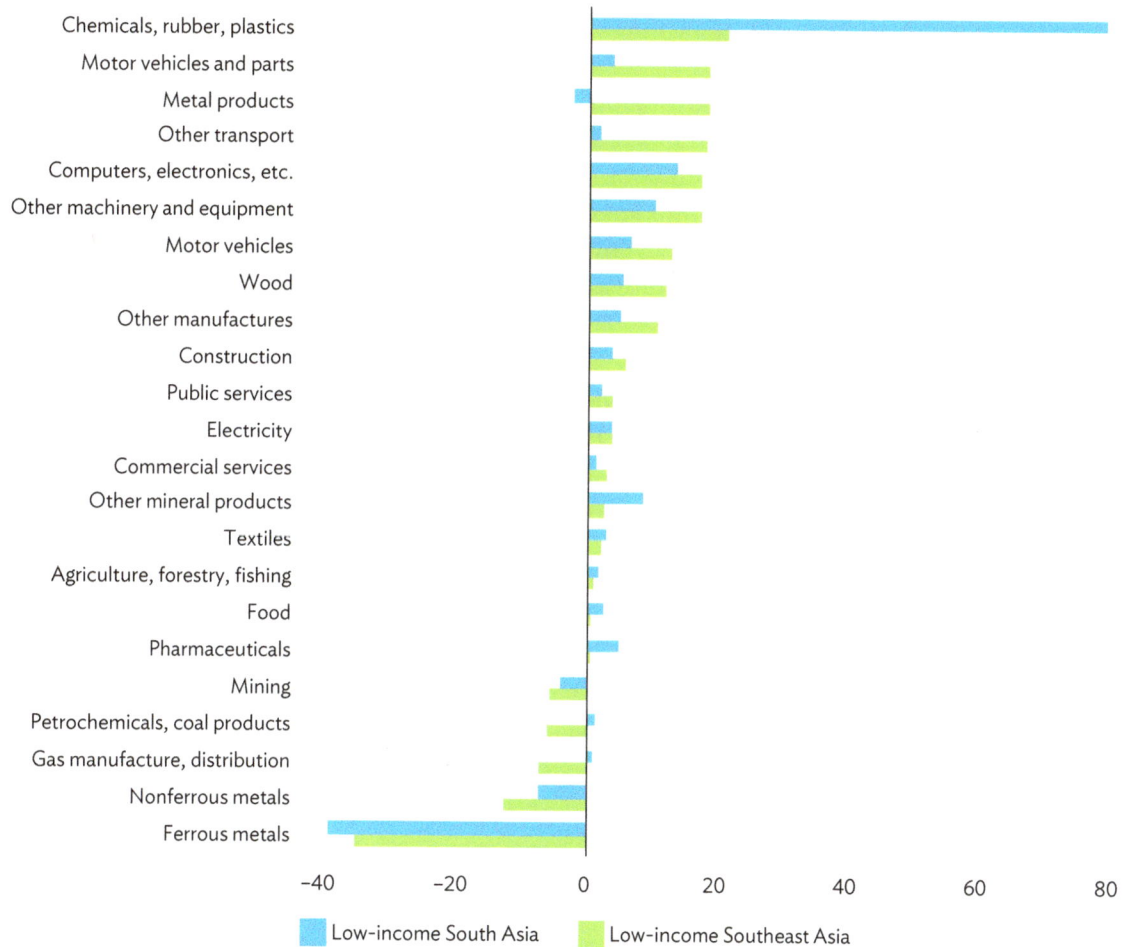

CBAM = Carbon Border Adjustment Mechanism, LDC = least developed country.
Sources: Global Trade Analysis Project 11 (https://www.gtap.agecon.purdue.edu/databases/v11/) and International Energy Agency
(https://www.iea.org/data-and-statistics) (both accessed 30 November 2023).

shift production in these sectors away from LDC Asia toward other countries in the region. Conversely, improvements in emissions-intensities in LDC Asia offsets some of the declines in output in these upstream sectors, suggesting that efforts to improve emissions-intensity through technology adoption can be an important force in maintaining competitiveness in upstream sectors for LDC Asia.

The largest estimated improvements in output are in chemicals as well as other, more downstream sectors such as computers, machinery, and motor vehicles. These changes are driven by a combination of emissions-intensity improvements in other Asian countries and in Asian LDCs themselves. As such, the results suggest that emissions efficiency improvements in other Asia can generate higher output in various downstream sectors in LDC Asia, with improvements in emissions-intensities in Asian LDCs enhancing output in upstream emissions-intensive sectors such as metals and chemicals.

Other Trade-Related Climate Measures

While CBAM has rightfully attracted a great deal of attention, it is not the only instrument by which economies seek to complement its own environmental rules with border measures. And like the CBAM, these other recent innovations may raise costs.

One example is the EU Deforestation Regulation (EUDR) that the EU adopted in 2023. This policy provides for restrictions on the importation of commodities that contribute to, or are produced, on land that was subjected to deforestation or forest degradation since 31 December 2020. Just as the CBAM can be seen as the border complement to the ETS, the EUDR is an extension of the EU Timber Regulation. It requires that exporting firms undertake due diligence along the entire supply chain by providing an assurance statement declaring that goods meet the EUDR requirements.

Seven commodity groups (including derived products) have thus far been identified as the most relevant drivers in deforestation or forest degradation: cattle, cocoa, coffee, palm, rubber, and timber.[33] Importers of these goods into the European Union need to provide for each product, among other things, descriptions, quantities, as well as geolocations, to ensure the traceability of its origin and processes along the supply chain. As in the case of CBAM, such record-keeping and reporting requirements are likely to increase trade costs; they may even preclude established exporters in some countries from continuing to supply the EU market. Numerous Asia and Pacific countries are exporters of affected products.

Similar issues arise with respect to the Corporate Sustainability Due Diligence Directive (CSDDD), which requires that companies engage in due diligence to prevent adverse human rights and environmental impacts in their own operations and across their value chains. As passed by the European Parliament on 1 April 2024, this directive places the onus on firms that supply the EU market, subject to certain thresholds. And like the other measures, it also follows on the heels of an otherwise local rule (namely the European Commission's guidance on due diligence for EU business published in July 2021). The CSDDD expands and replaces the previous EU legislation on environmental and social governance, entitled the Non-Financial Reporting Directive with the Corporate Sustainability Reporting Directive. In addition to drawing upon various human rights conventions,[34] the CSDDD deals with environmental issues. It does so by referencing breaches of the obligations that are delineated in such international environmental conventions as the 1992 Convention on Biological Diversity, the Convention on International Trade in Endangered Species of Wild Fauna and Flora, the Basel Convention, the Montreal Protocol, and the UNFCCC.

---

[33] See Table A5 in Appendix 1.
[34] These include the International Covenant on Civil and Political Rights, the Universal Declaration of Human Rights, and the International Covenant on Economic, Social and Cultural Rights.

The CSDDD seeks to harmonize EU member states' own supply chain measures so as to strengthen corporate due diligence on sustainability issues. It is thus not entirely new, as some Asia and Pacific exporters already have experience meeting the requirements previously set in the national laws of their EU partners. It nonetheless marks a significant departure from previous regimes that were voluntary. Noncompliance with the CSDDD will result in sanctions, and the directive's ambit encompasses both EU and third-country entities.

This directive could potentially affect almost any manufactures that are exported by Asia and Pacific economies, but it is especially stringent with respect to agriculture, mineral resources, and textiles. Those sectors are not subject to the thresholds that apply to all others, meaning that only relatively large firms are subject to these rules for other types of manufactures. There are thus two reasons why the CSDDD may be especially challenging for some of the poorest countries in the region: The sectors not subject to these thresholds tend to be especially prominent in low-income economies that depend either on primary products or on labor-intensive goods such as textiles, and these are also countries that are less likely to have in place the legal frameworks and mechanisms that will facilitate their compliance with the EU rules. New contractual arrangements may be needed to ensure that these requirements are embedded in GVCs. Governments can support this process through working with business associations and chambers of commerce.

Chapter 7

Green Technologies and Other Sectoral Solutions

Introduction

Technology is part of both the problem and the solution, whether one approaches this issue primarily from a trade or climate perspective. Seen as part of the problem, the Industrial Revolution created a production system built around the burning of fossil fuels, thus encouraging industrialization, developing intensive agricultural practices, and enabling rapid population growth; these were major factors that contributed to rising greenhouse gas (GHG) emissions and climate change. Seen as part of the solution, modern technological change serves to devise and diffuse green technologies. Innovations in new green energy technologies related to transportation, building, and energy distribution, for example, can have important effects on climate change mitigation, while innovations related to coastal protection, agriculture, human health, and infrastructure can help economies adapt to the effects of climate change. Many of the technologies needed to mitigate climate change are on the market; some of these are already offering superior quality at a lower price compared to existing nongreen technologies. That said, the scaling up of these technologies and their diffusion remains sluggish, especially for developing economies.

The sharing of technologies and goods is often a lifeline for countries dealing with both the acute problems of climate change and immediate disasters. It helps produce and provide critical goods and services in places where production facilities might be rendered inoperable by climate disasters. This is also the case with the provision of necessary technologies that reduce emissions without jeopardizing economic competitiveness. The *Asian Economic Integration Report 2023* (ADB 2023d) highlights the importance of trade in environmental goods to mitigate climate change in the region. Trade in environmental goods and services will also cut prices and improve access to green technologies.

On the Production and Diffusion of Green Technologies

One set of green technologies are those associated with the production of clean energy, including wind, solar, hydropower, geothermal, and bioenergy. Improvements in these technologies in recent years have led to rapid declines in the price per kilowatt hour, making them highly price-competitive relative to fossil fuels. The data in Figure 7.1 show the great strides that alternative, renewable energy sources made in cost reductions over just 1 decade. To reduce carbon dioxide (CO_2) emissions still further, these technologies will need to be scaled up and more widely diffused, with the choice of clean energy source adapted to the needs of specific economies.

Figure 7.1: Levelized Cost of Energy from Alternative Renewables, 2011–2021

(average cost per unit of energy generated across the lifetime of a new power plant, constant 2021 United States dollars per kilowatt-hour)

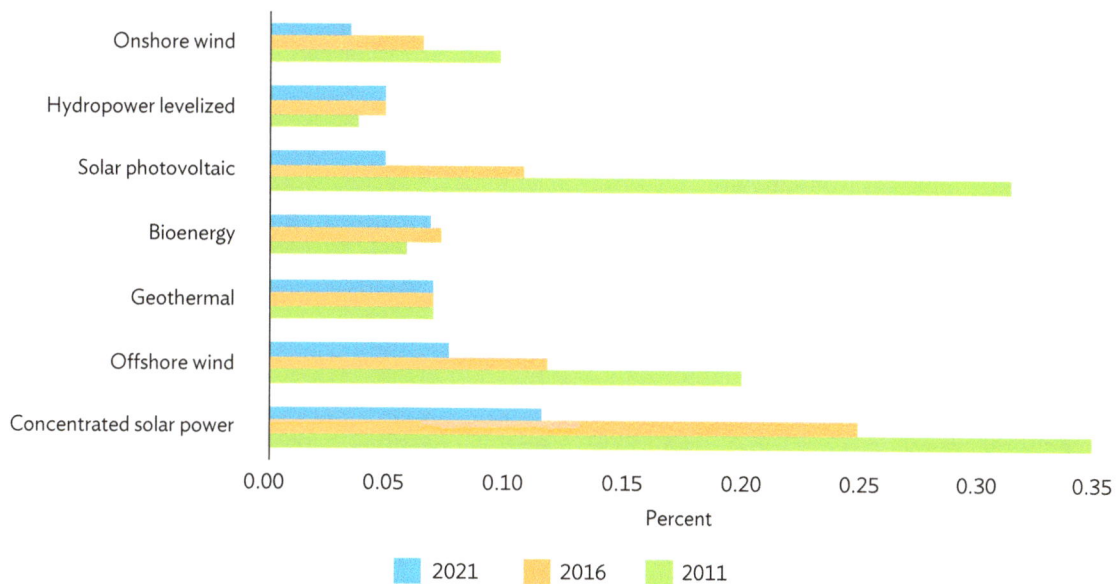

Source: Our World in Data. Levelized Cost of Energy by Technology. (https://ourworldindata.org/grapher/levelized-cost-of-energy).

These modes represent just a fraction of green technologies, a broad category that covers a wide variety of sectors and activities. Carbon-capture and -storage technologies address the legacy of past emissions, potentially removing carbon directly from the air and helping to clean dirty sectors. Other mitigation technologies are targeted at specific sectors (e.g., electric vehicles in transport, energy efficient heating in construction), and technologies associated with reducing emissions and waste in the production or processing of goods (e.g., emissions from cement production), waste management, and efforts to improve electrical power transmission, distribution, and usage. Precision agriculture based around digital technologies can reduce emissions from agricultural production, and developments in creating climate-resilient crops and improved soil carbon sequestration offers important means of adapting to climate change. Adaptation technologies are a further important component of green innovation, covering aspects such as conserving water, protecting infrastructure, preserving human health, and abating pollution.

The Concentration of Green Technology Innovation

Innovation tends to be heavily concentrated in a small number of economies, a point that is even more emphatic for green technologies. Table 7.1 shows the concentration of global patent applications by economy in which the invention took place, reporting the Herfindahl Index (a measure of concentration)[35] and the three- and five-economy concentration ratios (i.e., the share of the top three and five economies in patenting activity). The data underline how a few countries account for most inventions. Nearly 82% of all patents originated in only three, while just over 90% originated in five economies (which for this broadest case were the People's Republic of China [PRC], Japan, the United States, the Republic of Korea, and Germany).[36] The corresponding Herfindahl index is 0.39. For purposes of comparison, using data for 2022 from the World Bank's World Development Index, the Herfindahl Index for global GDP was 0.1, while the three- and five-economy concentration ratios were 47% and 55%, respectively. In short, patenting is more concentrated than GDP.

Green technologies accounted for around 13.2% of overall patenting over the period 2000–2022, mostly in mitigation (8.6%). In contrast, power generation (0.2%), adaptation technologies (1.3%), and environmental management (3.0%) took smaller shares of the total. The concentration of patenting for green technologies is even higher than for all technologies. The five-economy concentration ratio, for example, indicate that 93%–94% of green patents originate from just five economies. For most other economies, gaining access to green technologies requires diffusion through trade and foreign direct investment (FDI).

Table 7.1: Concentration of Patenting, 2000–2022

	Concentration of Invention			Concentration of Patenting by Economy of Application		
	Herfindahl Index	Three-Economy Concentration (%)	Five-Economy Concentration (%)	Herfindahl Index	Three-Economy Concentration (%)	Five-Economy Concentration (%)
All technologies	0.392	81.8	90.1	0.035	22.9	27.2
Green technologies	0.488	86.2	93.4	0.044	23.7	28.1
Mitigation	0.447	84.8	93.0	0.036	21.7	26.2
Adaptation	0.638	89.6	93.9	0.057	25.8	29.2
Environmental management	0.558	89.3	94.1	0.077	32.1	36.7
Power generation	0.437	83.4	93.1	0.045	54.7	58.3

Source: Authors' calculations from data of the European Patent Office's PATSTAT Database (2013 Autumn edition). (https://www.epo.org/en/searching-for-patents/business/patstat) (accessed 30 April 2024).

---

[35] The Herfindahl Index is constructed as the sum of the squared shares of each economy in patenting activity, with the index ranging between 0 and 1. Higher numbers indicate more concentrated patenting.

[36] Note that the specific composition of the "three-economy" and "five-economy" compositions shown in Table 7.1 will vary from group to another, such that while in some cases the top three will indeed be the PRC, Japan, and the United States this is not universally the case.

The heavy concentration of innovation in a small number of economies implies that developing economies contribute minimally. Table 7.2 reports information on the share of patents in all technologies and in green technologies from economies at different income levels. Low-income economies account for a tiny fraction of innovations, and lower-middle-income economies for less than 1% of all patents in the different technologies (and even fewer green patents). The upper-middle-income economies account for a substantial share of patents over the period 2000–2022, but this share is highly distorted by the fact that a single economy (the PRC) represents the vast majority of these patents.

The diffusion of green technologies is much less concentrated than their development and patenting. Originators of patents commonly patent their technologies in other economies, with the decision on where to patent linked to where the technologies are likely to be used and, therefore, where the risk of imitation is largest. Table 7.2 reports information on the concentration of patenting activity by application authority. Considering both the Herfindahl index and the two concentration ratios, the table reports substantially less concentration of patenting activity by destination than by origin of invention. In the case of all technologies, the three- and five-economy concentration ratios suggest that around 23% and 27% of patent applications are taken out in three and five economies, respectively. While still high, these numbers are substantially lower than for the origin of inventions.

For all green technologies, around 24% and 28% of patent applications are taken out in three and five economies, respectively, shares that are higher than for all technologies. There are also substantial differences in diffusion across types of green innovation The shares are substantially larger in the case of environmental management (32% and 37%, respectively) and power generation (55% and 58%, respectively) than for mitigation (22% and 26%, respectively) and adaptation (26% and 29%), suggesting lower diffusion of environmental management and power generation technologies on average.

Table 7.2: Distribution of Patent Applications by Income of Inventing Economy, 2000–2022
(%)

	Distribution of Inventions by Income				Share of Patent Applications by Income Level			
	Low	Lower Middle	Upper Middle	High	Low	Lower Middle	Upper Middle	High
All technologies	0.002	0.724	62.076	37.198	3.44	5.91	28.91	61.75
Green technologies	0.001	0.323	69.643	30.033	2.55	4.38	31.02	62.05
Mitigation	0.002	0.356	80.788	18.854	2.34	4.01	28.62	65.03
Adaptation	0.001	0.396	74.615	24.988	3.43	5.87	35.44	55.26
Environmental management	0.001	0.353	64.888	34.758	2.96	5.11	38.25	53.67
Power generation	0.001	0.294	66.104	33.600	1.88	3.16	30.72	64.24

Source: Authors' calculations from data of the European Patent Office's PATSTAT Database (2013 Autumn edition). (https://www.epo.org/en/searching-for-patents/business/patstat) (accessed 30 April 2024).

Few patent applications are taken out in lower-middle (6%) and low-income (3%) economies. This reflects such factors as differences in the number of economies within each income bracket, levels of consumption, rates of invention, and levels of development (and therefore imitative ability). More surprisingly, given the exposure of lower-income economies to climate change, is that lower-middle and low-income economies account for a smaller share of green patent applications than total applications.

Trade, Investment, and the Diffusion of Green Technologies

Trade is an important channel for the transfer of green technologies across borders, allowing economies to acquire the knowledge, expertise, and technologies that contribute to environmental sustainability. FDI can play an important role in diffusing green technologies by channeling capital, expertise, and technology transfer, creating links with local firms and other actors.

Imports and inward FDI are the main channels through which technology developed elsewhere will be supplied. As such, there is an expectation that higher imports and FDI will be associated with increased patenting. This is confirmed for green technologies in Figure 7.2, which reports the elasticity of green patent applications to various trade and investment indicators. The figure suggests that a 1% increase in imports in an economy is associated with a 0.49% increase in green patent applications, with a similar increase in imports of green goods associated with a 0.35% increase.[37] The different indicators of inward FDI—the value of FDI inflows, the number of greenfield FDI projects, and the number of merger and acquisition deals—also show a positive association with green patent applications, though associations tend to be somewhat smaller.

Figure 7.2 confirms that patent applications in different types of green technologies are strongly associated with imports and imports of green goods. The estimated elasticities are similar, with elasticities for total imports ranging from 0.47 to 0.52 and for green imports from 0.33 to 0.45. When considering total imports, elasticities tend to be somewhat larger for environmental management and adaptation technologies.

Technology Sharing Mechanisms

Beyond provisions in trade agreements, developed economies can support developing economies in other ways that rely on the removal of barriers to the diffusion and transfer of green technologies. Green technologies are often covered by intellectual property and the patenting of such technologies. While intending to encourage innovation, intellectual property rights can lead to increased market power for innovators, resulting in lower output and sales, and can add costs to others looking to access such technologies through licensing and other agreements. Such concerns can call for alternative systems and structures that result in more collaborative outcomes involving the pooling or sharing of technologies. Examples include patent pools, patent commons,

---

[37] The smaller coefficient on imports of green goods may reflect the relatively narrow definition of green goods in the APEC list of green products.

Figure 7.2: Estimated Responsiveness of Green Patent Applications to Indicators of Trade, by Type

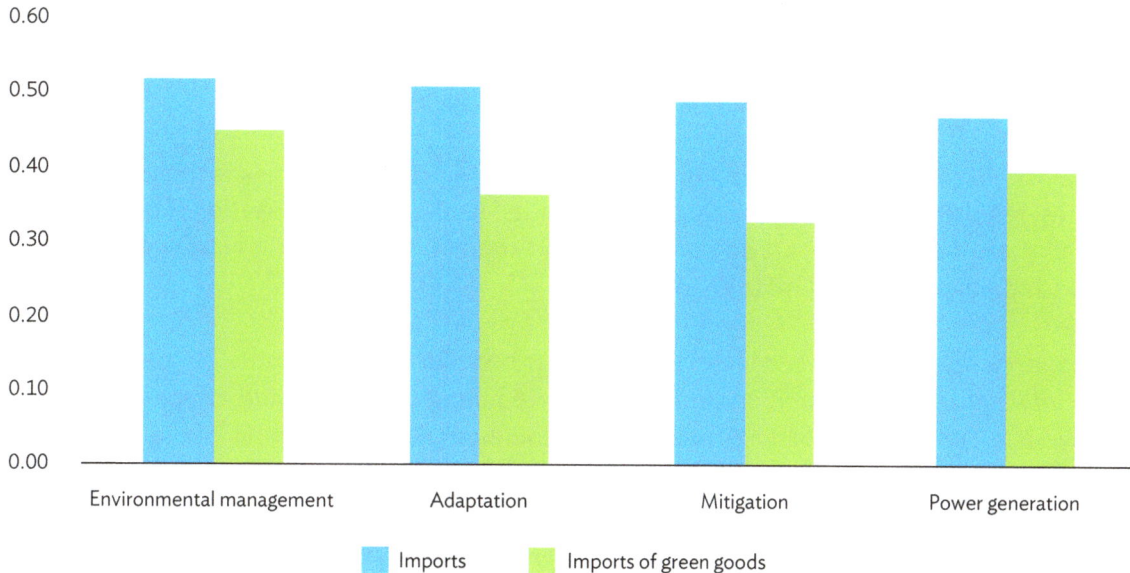

APEC = Asia-Pacific Economic Cooperation, FDI = foreign direct investment, GDP = gross domestic product.

Notes: Estimates of elasticities on trade variables from a Poisson regression model of the number of patent applications taken out in each of up to 190 economies over 2000–2022. In addition to the trade and FDI variables (included separately), the model includes the log of per capita GDP in constant US$ and the log of population (both averaged over the period 2000–2022). Green goods are defined according to the APEC (2012) list of green products at APEC. Annex C - APEC List of Environmental Goods. https://www.apec.org/meeting-papers/leaders-declarations/2012/2012_aelm/2012_aelm_annexc.

Source: Authors' calculations using the European Patent Office's PATSTAT Database (https://www.epo.org/en/searching-for-patents/business/patstat), UN Comtrade (https://comtrade.un.org/), FDi Markets, and World Development Indicators. (https://www.fdimarkets.com/) (accessed 31 May 2024).

open-source innovation, and open-licensing arrangements. While each of these have their own challenges, and there are questions about how best to organize and structure such initiatives and which technologies should be covered, they can be effective tools to diffuse green technologies to developing economies.

A patent pool is an agreement by multiple patent holders to share intellectual property among themselves, or to license a portfolio of patents as a package to outsiders. These are typically developed on a voluntary basis by technology holders, with the benefits being largely intended for those in the patent pool. While this approach may limit their role in facilitating green technology transfer to developing economies, open patent pools in which technologies can be accessed by any party could be more effective. A related approach is the use of patent commons, in which technology holders pledge their patented technologies for widespread use for no royalty payment. For example, the Eco-Patent Commons encourages firms to donate patents which, while not essential to their own business development, provide environmental benefits. Alternatively, developed economies could engage in international cooperation to pay licensing fees for green technologies, buying out the patents and assisting developing economies. While these options all have their advantages and disadvantages, the need is clear for policies and initiatives to assist in the diffusion of green technology to developing economies.

Technology Transfer and the Least Developed Countries

Access to technologies is critical for an inclusive global value chain (GVC) participation. New technologies and related knowledge spillovers can be made available not just to the local branches of multinational enterprises, but also to smaller firms allowing to strategically position themselves along the value chains.

There is a risk that least developed countries (LDCs) could be marginalized as technical change accelerates, left using outdated technologies with limited resources for innovation. This will compound the challenge of export diversification, and could hinder the role of trade to support mitigation and adaptation to climate change.

Some economies would like to see technology transfer on voluntary and mutually agreed terms between intellectual property holders and recipients, requiring open trade and investment regimes. LDCs have stressed the importance of technology generation and the potential of the Working Group on Transfer of Technology to support this. They point to the group's sharing of country experience, helping to identify how trade can facilitate technology transfer, and were keen to see greater links with the Trade-Related Aspects of Intellectual Property Rights (TRIPs) Council discussions, to enable the cross-fertilization of ideas.

LDC members have until 1 July 2034 to protect intellectual property under the World Trade Organization (WTO) Agreement on the TRIPs Agreement. Article 66.2 of that agreement requires that developed countries "provide incentives to enterprises and institutions in their territories for the purpose of promoting and encouraging technology transfer to LDC Members in order to enable them to create a sound and viable technological base." These flexibilities have enabled LDCs such as Bangladesh (now in the process of graduation) to develop pharmaceutical industries. Careful reflection on legal and regulatory frameworks is required. The most recent briefing by the United Nations Technology Executive Committee found that these frameworks help LDCs consider how their technology needs assessments under the United Nations Framework Convention on Climate Change (UNFCCC) processes are currently being met (economic and finance enablers come first, followed by information and awareness).

The United Nations Technology Executive Committee concludes that support to programs designed to strengthen the developing countries' institutional and scientific capacities with regard to technology development and transfer is critical to creating the long-term enabling environments required for technology development and transfer. Governments have a major role to play in creating enabling environments and enforcing the appropriate regulatory and institutional framework. Most developing country parties identified the creation of enabling environments in the economic and finance sectors through regulations and policies as necessary to assist with the development and transfer of new technologies.

Improving Conditions for Green Technological Innovation and Diffusion

Developing economies need to improve their innovation capacity in green technologies, adapting existing technologies and developing new ones that serve their needs. Support for capacity-building and technical assistance will be crucial in enabling developing economies to enhance their capabilities in green technologies and allowing them to benefit from imported green technologies and potentially develop as a destination for green FDI. This will include the building of the skills and knowledge in the workforce to enable the absorption of green technologies as well as efforts to enhance the local scientific and technical knowledge. Domestic regulatory policies that support investment can encourage technology transactions. Policies related to intellectual property can facilitate technological development and diffusion. Access to finance and investment is a major constraint to innovation and the diffusion and adoption of technology globally, calling for increased climate finance.

Developing economies can become partners in the co-development of green technologies. Through such partnerships, including joint ventures, collaborative research and development (R&D), and technology collaboration programs, opportunities for technology development enables the adaptation of green technologies to local contexts and supporting innovation. Regional value chains and GVCs offer an opportunity for developing countries to participate by supplying not only final goods, but also other intermediate products and components and services related to environmental goods and services. Developing countries producing less technology-intensive and intermediate products and components could contribute to the manufacture of environmental products as part of their GVCs.

A Case Study: Solar Photovoltaic Systems

Solar photovoltaic (PV) power generation technologies illustrate the potential benefits. A recent study by Wang et al. (2021) found that liberalizing PV trade could yield substantial reductions in carbon emissions by stimulating production, reducing prices and application costs, and expanding power capacity. Improvements in environmental technologies are propelled by economies of scale, innovation, and the emergence of GVCs. Enhancements in the advancement and utilization of energy-efficient technology and manufacturing expand power generation while reducing the cost of electricity (Figure 7.3).

Figure 7.3: Average Prices for Solar Photovoltaic Modules and Electricity Generation, 2010–2022

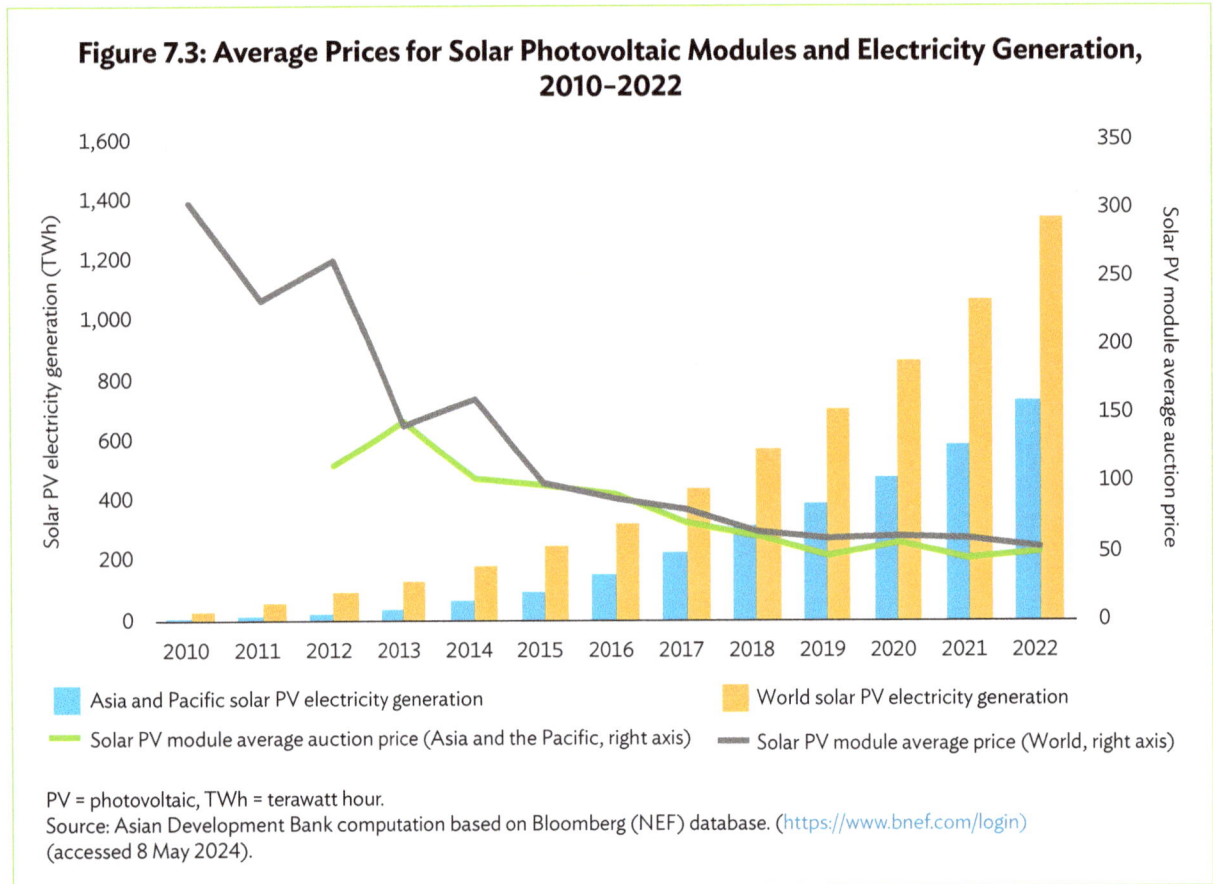

PV = photovoltaic, TWh = terawatt hour.
Source: Asian Development Bank computation based on Bloomberg (NEF) database. (https://www.bnef.com/login) (accessed 8 May 2024).

The PRC and Viet Nam are major suppliers in this market (Table 7.3). Viet Nam offers a true success story, with the government's dedication to energy security playing a pivotal role. Do et al. (2020) applied an economic, social, and institutional framework, revealing that the government's strategy of implementing attractive solar feed-in tariffs (FITs) aimed at fostering solar power generation played a pivotal role. Other government policies also mattered, such as flexibility in accessing finance as well as tariff and tax exemptions, helping manufacturers to vertically integrate upstream and downstream domestic solar manufacturing and in broadening their GVC participation. Mekong countries (Myanmar, Thailand, and Cambodia) have significant solar power potential, and can learn from Viet Nam's success by focusing on reforming regulations and building capacity to enhance competitiveness.

Table 7.3: Top 10 Economies' Solar Photovoltaic Total Trade and Value Chain Component Installed Capacity

	2012			2022		Manufacturing Capacity (2022)				
	Total Trade ($ million)	Share in World (%)		Total Trade ($ million)	Share in World (%)	Polysilicon (MT)	Ingot (MW)	Wafer (MW)	Cell (MW)	Module (MW)
1. PRC	23,916	25.5	1. PRC	58,520	68.8	939,500	458,105	478,491	460,788	542,519
2. Japan	8,935	9.5	2. Viet Nam	10,901	12.8	–	4,000	4,000	18,000	26,325
3. Republic of Korea	6,910	7.4	3. Hong Kong, China	7,423	8.7	–	–	–	–	–
4. Hong Kong, China	3,528	3.8	4. Japan	6,544	7.7	11,400	–	330	1,363	1,532
5. Malaysia	2,896	3.1	5. Republic of Korea	6,075	7.1	6,500	150	50	7,876	10,030
6. Singapore	2,314	2.5	6. Singapore	4,607	5.4	–	–	833	1,500	1,800
7. Australia	1,028	1.1	7. Malaysia	4,503	5.3	35,000	600	800	16,150	14,880
8. India	984	1.0	8. Thailand	4,107	4.8	–	–	–	16,300	10,412
9. Thailand	814	0.9	9. India	2,132	2.5	–	2	77	3,627	14,527
10. Viet Nam	351	0.4	10. Australia	1,643	1.9	–	–	–	–	–
World	**93,756**	**100.0**	**World**	**85,074**	**100.0**	**1,128,385**	**468,872**	**491,773**	**538,442**	**656,505**

PRC = People's Republic of China, MT = metric ton, MW = megawatt.
Note: "Total Trade" is the sum of exports plus imports.
Source: Asian Development Bank calculations based on World Integrated Trade Solutions (WITS) Database for Trade and Bloomberg (NEF) Database for Manufacturing Capacity.

The benefits of PV production can extend up and down the value chain. The key upstream components of a PV system include silica, polysilicon, ingot, and wafer, while its downstream components include PV cell, PV module/panel, and integration of the PV system. A solar panel requires such mineral-based raw materials as copper, aluminum, silver, lithium, and nickel. In a globally/regionally competitive structure, the entire list of raw materials and components cannot be produced locally, thus producing an opportunity for developing countries to identify areas where they have a comparative advantage.

Several countries in the region are endowed with essential minerals required for PV manufacturing. Cambodia and the Lao People's Democratic Republic (Lao PDR) have the potential for bauxite extraction, which can be further refined into aluminum; Papua New Guinea already produces bauxite and hopes to expand participation in the value chain. Mekong countries boast ample supplies of silicon, the primary raw material used in solar PV production. Indonesia contributes about half of the global nickel supply, yet processes only about 15% of it, and so hopes to play a larger role. To that end, the country banned exports of raw nickel in 2020. While the ban has significantly bolstered the domestic industry, it also posed challenges in negotiations for free trade and investment agreements, thereby limiting opportunities for both Indonesia and its potential partners (Vekasi 2023).

The PV sector's mineral requirements are poised for substantial expansion. Projections from the International Energy Agency's (IEA) Roadmap to Net Zero Emissions by 2050 indicate that silver demand for solar PV manufacturing in 2030 could surpass 30% of the total global silver output, and copper demand in 2030 may triple from its 2020 level (IEA 2021 and IEA 2022). With silicon prices rising, the price of solar PV modules increased for the first time after a decade of declining prices (IEA 2023). Diversifying the critical minerals market with countries having potential for mining raw materials will not just meet rising demand for critical minerals, but could reduce price volatility. This provides opportunities for developing countries to leverage the interconnectedness of extraction, distribution, and marketing of PV raw materials through GVCs and transition toward a more sustainable, low-carbon energy system.

Although mineral extraction requires significant energy, efforts have been made to minimize electricity usage. For example, APEC economies formed a Mining Task Force in 2007, emphasizing key principles such as enhancing the information and policy landscape, employing a multi-stakeholder approach, and embracing sustainable and inclusive development strategies. In 2018, the ministerial group responsible for mining convened in Papua New Guinea and outlined an agenda for inclusive and sustainable mining in the region. This agenda underscores the importance of the broader value chain and the mining equipment, technology, and services sector in driving employment, growth, and innovation, highlighting their integral role in the mining, energy, and resources industry (APEC 2018). In terms of emission intensities, carbon emissions from PV manufacturing surged nearly fourfold with increased production and demand expanded in 2021 (IEA 2022). Nonetheless, rising emissions are offset by improvements in energy and material efficiency, as well as decreasing emissions from electricity generation.

Chapter 8

Translating Climate Challenges into Aid for Trade Opportunities

Conclusion

As the world grapples with the twin challenges of economic development and climate change, the Asia and Pacific region finds itself at the heart of a critical transition. The Aid for Trade (AfT) initiative, a pivotal tool in this transformation, serves not only as a mechanism for enhancing trade capacity and infrastructure but also as a conduit for environmental sustainability. The evidence presented in this report underscores the integral role that AfT can play in promoting sustainable trade practices that align with the broader objectives of climate policy.

This report has highlighted several key areas where AfT has effectively supported the region's adaptation to and mitigation of climate change. By bolstering infrastructure, facilitating access to green technologies, and fostering an inclusive policy environment, AfT initiatives have laid a foundation for sustainable economic growth. However, the varying impacts across different subregions and the diverse needs of developing member countries underscore the necessity for targeted and nuanced approaches.

The report discusses the critical role of multilateral cooperation and regional integration in achieving the Sustainable Development Goals. By participating in and shaping multilateral, regional, and bilateral trade agreements that include environmental considerations, the Asia and Pacific region can leverage collective action for greater environmental and economic outcomes. In addition, ongoing discussions on environmental goods and services (EGS) within the trade frameworks of the Asia and Pacific economies is a testament to the region's commitment to sustainable development. EGS trade, coupled with environmental provisions in trade agreements, not only have the potential to address the climate challenge but also to open new avenues for economic diversification and resilience building. The uneven distribution of gains nonetheless calls for careful design and use of environmental and trade policy instruments, and for a balanced approach between environmental sustainability and short-term trade competitiveness, to ensure that all nations can benefit from green trade.

The evolving landscape of global climate policy, including mechanisms such as the Carbon Border Adjustment Mechanism (CBAM), presents challenges as well as opportunities. For the Asia and Pacific economies, navigating these changes is paramount to securing their trade interests and economic sovereignty. The report demonstrates the need for these economies to enhance their policy frameworks not only to face the external challenges posed by such mechanisms, but also to harness the potential of green technologies and industries for domestic growth and development.

It is imperative that policymakers continue integrating climate considerations into trade policies and AfT frameworks. Investments should be strategically directed toward projects that offer the dual benefits of trade enhancement and environmental protection. The region should promote an inclusive economic environment that enables all stakeholders, especially micro, small, and medium-sized enterprises (MSMEs), to participate in and benefit from trade.

Further research and adaptation of strategies will be necessary to address the emerging challenges and harness new opportunities presented by the global transition toward sustainability. The AfT initiative must evolve, incorporating lessons learned and adapting to the changing global landscape to continue its role as a catalyst for sustainable development in Asia and the Pacific. AfT also aims for gender equality in its programs to ensure female-run businesses have equal access to finance, technologies, and market opportunities. It can support marginalized communities, such as businesses owned by people with disabilities, with financial products, capacity-building, and market access opportunities.

Policy Options

AfT strategies can play a pivotal role in transforming these challenges into sustainable trade opportunities. This section outlines actionable policy options to enhance the synergy between climate actions and trade competitiveness, focusing on policy alignment, access to climate finance, and leveraging trade for environmental sustainability.

Aligning National Trade Strategies with Climate Actions

Enhancing Coordination Between Trade and Environmental Ministries

Enhancing coordination between trade and environmental ministries is essential to creating synergistic policies that support both economic growth and environmental protection.

(i) **Develop integrated policy frameworks.** AfT can encourage the development of integrated policy frameworks that explicitly include sustainability and climate resilience as core components of trade policies and economic development plans. Such frameworks will help align national trade policies and objectives with nationally determined contributions (NDCs) and National Adaptation Programmes of Action (NAPAs). The success of such initiatives will depend on the degree of coordination across ministries. AfT can be used to foster such coordination through the establishment of dedicated interministerial and public–private committees to ensure that national trade strategies are designed with strong environmental foresight.

(ii) **Conduct interministerial policy development workshops and training programs.** Regular workshops and policy labs should be held to facilitate the integration of trade and environmental priorities into coherent policy documents and national strategies that reflect both sustainable trade and environmental protection. Collaborative training programs for the stakeholders of both ministries will encourage a common understanding of the challenges and opportunities inherent in both domains.

(iii) **Leverage technology and data-sharing between the ministries.** The lack of data remains a central challenge in many countries. Even when data are available, a lack of sharing between ministries will complicate evidence-based policymaking. AfT could assist with developing interoperable systems for trade and climate data collection, and support the establishment of mechanisms for the effective data exchange to improve policy-level design and outcomes.

(iv) **Harmonize performance metrics.** While both ministries have targets for the impact of their policies, they often exist without consideration of their interaction. A joint development of performance metrics between the trade and environment ministries would improve synergies by providing a suitable tool for the measurement of the impact of integrated policymaking.

Raising Capacities for Climate Policy Integration

The integration of climate resilience and low-carbon technologies into national trade strategies and industrial policies should support sectors that are both trade-intensive and vulnerable to climate impacts. To help the process, AfT can fund capacity-building programs for policymakers and trade negotiators to understand climate issues deeply, and integrate them into trade negotiations and agreements. The AfT initiative can also help establish platforms for sharing best practices in climate-smart trade policies among developing countries.

Selected Regional Best Practices

The Asia Pacific Adaptation Network supports capacity-building efforts and national policy formulation. Several countries in the region have also adopted dedicated ministries or governmental bodies to address climate change, which also collaborate with ministries involved in the development of trade strategies. Examples include the following:

- **Fiji.** The Ministry of Waterways and the Environment includes climate change in its portfolio; other efforts include easing business and increasing trade facilitation, to ensure risk reduction and environmental protection objectives and actions can be interlinked and collectively addressed (Ministry of Economy, Republic of Fiji 2021).

- **Indonesia.** The Ministry of Environment and Forestry deals with climate change; the Climate Change Development Report indicates a structured approach to embedding climate action within policy frameworks; Indonesia is also part of the Assessing Low Carbon Transition initiative, having recently published a report on Green Trade (2024).

- **Singapore.** The Ministry of Sustainability and the Environment is responsible for climate change policies; the Green Plan of 2021 focuses on increasing sustainability, cutting carbon emissions, promoting job and investment opportunities, and increasing climate resilience and food security. New Memoranda of Understanding with the United Kingdom and the United States seek to support Singapore's green economy development.

Examples of Aid for Trade Projects in the Region

Regarding specific AfT projects in the region to support the greening of trade, Kazakhstan, the Kyrgyz Republic, Tajikistan, Turkmenistan, and Uzbekistan all work with the United Nations Environment Programme to address barriers and facilitate the transfer of clean technology. One example of AfT supporting green productive capacities is the project Aid for Trade in Central Asia.[38] It seeks to enhance green productive capacities and competitiveness, supporting export diversification, through such activities as supporting MSMEs and promoting trade along green and niche value chains.

Accessing Climate Financing Through Aid for Trade and Public–Private Partnerships

Leveraging Aid for Trade for Climate Projects

AfT can be strategically used to develop projects that link climate resilience with trade infrastructure. Initiatives such as green ports and eco-friendly industrial zones can attract significant climate finance. Enhancing coordination among bilateral and multilateral donors is crucial to ensure that climate finance and AfT complement each other, minimizing redundancy and maximizing impact. Simplifying the application processes for accessing climate finance from international funds, such as the Green Climate Fund and the Global Environment Facility, can further facilitate the integration of trade and climate objectives. AfT can provide the necessary technical assistance to developing countries and least developed countries (LDCs) for developing robust funding applications.

Enhancing Donor Coordination and Facilitating Climate Financing Access

Improving donor coordination can lead to more effective use of resources and greater impact. By working closely with international climate funds to simplify bureaucratic hurdles, developing countries and LDCs can more easily access climate finance. In addition, AfT funds can play a pivotal role by offering technical assistance and capacity-building support, ensuring that countries have the skills and knowledge to navigate the complexities of international climate finance mechanisms, and can prepare effective funding proposals that meet international criteria. This support can lead to more successful applications and better implementation of climate-related trade projects.

Leveraging Private Sector Investments Through Policy Advocacy and Public–Private Partnerships

Developing financial instruments and incentives for the private sector to invest in climate-resilient trade infrastructure and green technologies is crucial. This can include risk guarantees and cofinancing options that make investments more attractive. International forums provide platforms to advocate for greater climate finance on trade-related adaptation and mitigation projects. Emphasizing the critical role of trade in climate action can help secure more support and funding. Public–private partnerships (PPPs) can play a significant role in financing and implementing projects

---

[38]   UNDP Europe and Central Asia. Aid for Trade in Central Asia. https://www.undp.org/eurasia/projects/aid-trade-central-asia.

that combine trade competitiveness with climate resilience. By encouraging PPPs, countries can leverage private sector expertise and resources to achieve more sustainable and impactful outcomes.

Supporting Economies to Mitigate and Adapt to Climate Change and Policy Dynamics

Conduct Careful Ex Ante Assessments of Climate Measures

AfT could fund detailed ex ante impact assessments to determine where climate measures are required to address social concerns and ensure a just transition. AfT can also fund such analysis in economies potentially affected by these measures to advocate for a transition phase.

Promoting Green Technologies and Renewable Energy

AfT can promote the adoption and diffusion of green technologies in developing economies, supporting their efforts to mitigate and adapt to climate change. By providing financial and technical assistance, AfT can facilitate the transition to lower-emission technologies in manufacturing and production processes through transfer of advanced green technologies to trade-focused industries, enabling these sectors to reduce their carbon footprints and enhance environmental sustainability. This support can encompass grants and subsidies for the acquisition of renewable energy systems (e.g., solar panels, energy-efficient kilns, and waste heat recovery systems), energy-efficient machinery, and waste management technologies. Increasing the provision of green investment funds that offers low-interest loans to companies investing in green technologies, in collaboration with technology providers, could further incentivize adoption. An initiative could include a partnership between international financial institutions and technology providers to offer deferred payment plans for green technology adoption, coupled with technical assistance programs to help companies implement and maintain these technologies effectively.

Recent reductions in renewable energy costs present an opportunity for "no regret" climate action in the power sector. Transitioning to low-carbon energy sources can reduce greenhouse gas emissions and save costs, while preventing the lock-in of emissions-intensive production and future asset stranding.

Creating an Enabling Domestic Regulatory Framework for the Development of Green Sectors

Domestic regulatory policies play a critical role in technology adoption and innovation. These include investment and intellectual property policies designed to facilitate technology development and diffusion while promoting local and foreign green investments.

Fostering Partnerships for Green Innovation

Given improvements in local innovation capabilities, developing economies can become partners in the co-development of green technologies. AfT can facilitate partnerships, including joint ventures, collaborative research and development (R&D), and technology collaboration programs. These partnerships can open up opportunities for local technology development, enabling the adaptation of green technologies to local contexts and supporting local innovation that serves the needs of developing economies. AfT can support capacity-building programs that enhance local scientific and technical knowledge, contributing to the development of new green solutions.

Supporting the Establishment of Carbon Markets

AfT can facilitate the establishment of carbon markets in developing economies through several concrete actions. AfT can fund the development of robust regulatory frameworks to ensure transparent and efficient market operations and provide technical assistance for setting up the necessary infrastructure for emissions measurement, reporting, and verification systems. Capacity-building initiatives for policymakers and market participants can be conducted to enhance understanding and management of carbon trading. Additionally, AfT can support regional cooperation in carbon trading to enhance market liquidity and stability. By assisting in the establishment of carbon markets and ensuring accurate emissions measurement, AfT helps developing countries monetize their emissions reductions, attract climate finance, and promote low-carbon economic growth.

Promoting Environmental Goods and Services Trade and Decarbonizing Value Chains

Fostering trade in environmental goods and services (EGS) can accelerate the transition toward lower-carbon systems, reducing pollution, and in meeting international climate change commitments. Reducing trade and investment barriers reduces the cost of inputs, enhances production of environmental goods and services, and expands the market availability of these goods and services. AfT can advance the liberalization of EGS in the integration in the following ways:

(i)   Assessing the liberalizing, regulatory, and economic benefits of integrating environmental sustainability in trade agreements;

(ii) AfT capacity-building programs could be developed to help countries adjust and effectively implement environment-related disciplines and commitments that are increasingly covered in new generation trade agreements such as the Comprehensive and Progressive Agreement for Trans-Pacific Partnership (CPTPP);

(iii) Build up negotiation and implementation capacity in negotiating trade and cooperation initiatives such as Green Economy Agreements;

(iv) AfT programming could promote policy-aimed research, capacity building, and implementing mechanisms to reduce the adverse impact of tariff and nontariff barriers to environmental goods and services; and

(v) With the awareness that trade in services has been left behind and given lesser attention compared to trade in goods, AfT can assist economies in achieving clearer, more transparent, and more facilitative services regulatory landscape in the region.

Aid for Trade to Support Developing Asian Economies Adapt to BCAs

Border Carbon Adjustments (BCAs), such as the European Union's Carbon Border Adjustment Mechanism (CBAM) put a price on carbon emissions associated with the production of imported goods, thereby encouraging cleaner production methods globally. However, for many developing Asian economies, adapting to these new requirements involves significant hurdles, including technical, financial, and capacity constraints. AfT can play a pivotal role in helping these economies meet CBAM and other future BCA requirements, thus promoting sustainable development and equitable trade practices.[39]

Enhancing Capacity and Infrastructure for Embedded Emissions Accounting and Reporting

AfT can significantly enhance the ability of businesses in developing Asian economies to meet European Union (EU) CBAM reporting requirements by funding and organizing workshops and capacity-building programs tailored to the needs of small and medium-sized enterprises (SMEs) in sectors most affected by CBAM. Developing partnerships with local universities and international environmental nongovernment organizations can help create training modules on carbon footprint calculation and environmental auditing. For example, regional centers of excellence could offer certification programs in emissions accounting and environmental compliance and management systems, serving as hubs for capacity building and the dissemination of best practices and technologies in emissions measurement. AfT could fund capacity-building for broader public and private audiences, creating dedicated emissions-accounting bodies with transparent governance frameworks, based on sound legal and regulatory frameworks that align with international standards.

This assistance should be complemented by AfT infrastructure support, including on the development of robust data-collection systems and information technology infrastructure necessary for data storage, processing, and analysis. These systems must be interoperable to ensure consistency and reliability. Financial assistance and incentive programs can support the initial setup and ongoing management of these systems. Funding should also cover the establishment of monitoring systems, pilot projects to test and refine methodologies, and research initiatives focused on improving emissions accounting technologies and practices. Public awareness campaigns and stakeholder engagement are essential to ensure widespread participation and transparency in emissions accounting efforts.

---

[39] The EU provides support measures to help developing and LDCs adapt to CBAM requirements, including technical assistance and capacity-building. See CBAM and Developing Countries, https://taxation-customs.ec.europa.eu/document/download/7abe56cc-4af0-490d-90e1-0a0825aabe37_en?filename=CBAM%20and%20developing%20countries.pdf.

Short-Term and Long-Term Assistance

While short-term assistance is necessary to help producers meet immediate CBAM reporting requirements, it is equally important to provide long-term technical and financial support to accelerate the green transition. Suppliers who have not begun their green transition by the time emission levies are introduced in 2026 may struggle to absorb the carbon costs and remain in the EU market. Therefore, a comprehensive approach that includes both immediate capacity-building and sustained support for green technology adoption is crucial. CBAM-affected industries may need sustained financial support.

Creating a multilateral fund focused on long-term investments in green infrastructure, such as renewable energy projects and carbon-capture and -storage facilities, can drive substantial emission reductions. Governments of CBAM-affected countries and their industries can partner with international development banks to offer favorable financing for large-scale green projects is essential. An example might include funding the construction of geothermal power plants or large-scale reforestation initiatives through partnerships with international financial institutions.

Market Access and Diversification Support

To help producers find alternative markets or diversify their product lines and reduce dependence on the EU market, AfT can assist in market research and the establishment of trade relationships or formal agreements. Organizing trade fairs and virtual business-matching events can facilitate these new connections.

Policy Advocacy and Dialogue Facilitation

Funding and facilitating ongoing dialogues between Asian governments and policymakers from regions implementing BCAs, such as the EU, the United Kingdom, and others to come, to negotiate lower BCA rates for a transition period or exemptions for certain sectors or products could help ensure a smoother transition. Establishing a multi-stakeholder platform that includes representatives from Asian economies, officials from BCA-implementing regions, and environmental experts for regular discussions of BCAs' impact and potential adjustments can lead to more equitable outcomes. For example, a policy advocacy group could draft and promote policy briefs highlighting the economic and environmental benefits of flexible BCA terms for developing countries, supplemented by high-level forums for stakeholder discussions.

Leveraging CBAM Revenue for Aid for Trade in CBAM Implementation

Using CBAM revenue to support sustainable development initiatives in exporting countries, particularly those in developing regions, would be fair and responsible. CBAM revenues could be channeled to aid developing country exporters, enabling them to meet environmental standards. Establishing a dedicated fund under the AfT framework, managed by a multilateral organization or regional development banks, can provide targeted support programs for sectors most affected by CBAM. These programs would offer technical assistance, technology transfer, and financial support to reduce emissions and enhance competitiveness.

To ensure equitable distribution, mechanisms should be designed to prioritize countries with the least capacity to reduce emissions. Establishing transparent governance structures for the fund can ensure that the revenue is used effectively, and that donor and recipient countries can hold it accountable. Strengthening international cooperation can ensure broad support for this initiative, facilitating dialogue between countries implementing CBAMs and those affected by them.

Integrating Climate Change into Aid for Trade Programs

Integrating climate change into the AfT program involves considering the policy options discussed above to enhance climate resilience and sustainability within the standard AfT categories: infrastructure, productive capacities, and trade policy and regulations. This integration aims to ensure that trade developments contribute to climate action while promoting economic growth. The following sections provide specific recommendations on how AfT can be designed and oriented to support these goals.

Climate-Resilient Infrastructure

AfT disbursements should focus on enhancing port facilities, roads, and logistical chains to withstand extreme weather conditions. Implementing stringent standards and guidelines for climate-resilient projects ensures adherence to best practices for sustainability and resilience. Dedicated funding mechanisms, or increased allocations within existing funds, are essential to prioritize climate-resilient infrastructure projects, especially in regions most vulnerable to climate impacts. PPPs can leverage private sector investment and expertise, promoting long-term sustainability in infrastructure development. This collaborative approach ensures that the infrastructure built today will be capable of handling the climatic challenges of tomorrow.

Enhancing Productive Capacities

AfT programs can facilitate the transition to green practices by providing targeted financial and technical support to businesses. Incentives such as tax breaks, subsidies, or grants for companies that reduce their carbon footprint or invest in sustainable technologies can drive the adoption of green practices. Offering grants for research and innovation in green technologies supports the development of new sustainable products and processes, fostering a green transformation in value chains.

Capacity-building initiatives should offer regular training programs, workshops, and seminars on climate change adaptation, mitigation, and sustainable trade practices should be organized for government officials, business leaders, and community representatives in developing and least developed countries. Establishing platforms for knowledge exchange and best practice sharing among these countries fosters collaboration and mutual learning in green trade and climate resilience.

Trade Policy and Regulations

Trade policies must incorporate environmental considerations into trade agreements, negotiations, and national trade strategies, while acknowledging the specific circumstances and development levels of different countries. Incorporating appropriate environmental standards and commitments in trade agreements and broadening their country coverage can help prevent environmental degradation without imposing undue burdens on developing countries. Regular climate impact assessments of trade policies and projects would help identify potential risks and mitigation measures, ensuring trade development aligns with climate-resilience goals.

Capacity-building efforts should extend to the policy sphere, equipping policymakers with the knowledge and skills necessary to integrate environmental considerations into trade policies effectively. Training programs for government officials and regulators on the intersection of trade and climate policy can ensure that environmental considerations are adequately reflected in trade agreements and strategies.

Integrating Climate and Trade Strategies for LDCs

Given the imperative of structural economic transformation for LDCs first to adapt to and then mitigate climate change, and also within timeframes recognized by the international community, it will be important to avoid limiting the use of old technologies and processes without considering proper transition measures. AfT should help LDCs maintain or enhance their trade competitiveness with long-term support to adapt to new trading conditions. Diagnostic trade integration studies (DTISs)/updates or their equivalent should refer to and draw on nationally determined contributions (NDCs) and National Adaptation Programmes of Action (NAPAs) and integrate climate effects. Conversely, NDCs and NAPAs should also consider trade effects. This could be a key element for inclusion within a successor program to the EIF. For graduating LDCs, both climate and trade must be integrated within national transition strategies.

There will be a need to ensure continuity of AfT and climate finance support post-graduation. While the EIF has recognized this need, such recognition is less evident for the provision of climate finance. To overcome some of these challenges and improve access to climate finance, the following recommendations should be considered:

- Mandated coordination between the providers of trade-related assistance and climate adaptation and mitigation finance;

- A consistent program of support to facilitate interactions between climate and trade negotiators and technical leads; and

- Making resources contingent on cross-collaboration between trade and climate negotiators and technical leads to break down the barriers that often exist between these two groups.

Tailored Programs Based on Stakeholders Consultation

Donor support should be tailored to the specific capabilities and needs of individual countries, in particular LDCs. Stakeholder consultations with representatives from affected industries, civil society, and the public sector can ensure that different actors' objectives are adequately represented in climate policy packages.

Monitoring and Evaluation

Robust monitoring and evaluation mechanisms are essential to assess the impact of AfT programs on climate resilience and sustainability. Developing frameworks for impact assessment, implementing regular reporting mechanisms, and establishing feedback systems from stakeholders, including local communities, ensure continuous improvement and accountability. Regular evaluations and assessments help track progress and effectiveness, facilitating informed decision-making and adjustments as needed. This continuous feedback loop ensures that AfT programs remain effective and responsive to both trade and climate challenges.

Appendix: Special Categories of Goods and Services

Carbon Border Adjustment Mechanism Product Coverage

The Carbon Border Adjustment Mechanism (CBAM) will initially cover six product groups considered to be at high risk of carbon leakage due to their energy intensity and tradability: aluminum, iron and steel, cement, fertilizers, hydrogen, and electricity.

What was left open in the original proposal was the exact definition of the product groups. Hydrogen and electricity posed no problems as they are defined by unique 8-digit codes in the Combined Nomenclature, which is used to classify goods for customs and statistical purposes. The four other groups were more difficult to delineate as they are made up of a large number of different products at 8-digit level.

Take steel as an example. Steel is produced by two processes: the blast furnace-basic oxygen furnace process, which uses iron ore, coke and electricity as the main inputs, and the electric arc furnace process, which melts recycled steel scrap to make new steel. The former is known as "primary steel" and the latter as "secondary steel," and both are covered by the CBAM as they emit large amounts of carbon dioxide (CO_2) as a by-product, particularly the former which uses coke as a reducing agent. The question was whether fabricated steel products should also be covered, such as flat-rolled stainless steel for the automotive industry and bars, rods, wires, tubes and pipes for the construction sector.

There were two arguments for including fabricated products, even though the fabrication stage itself emits relatively little CO_2 compared to the primary stage. First, if fabricated steel products were excluded, CBAM could be circumvented by processing the primary steel into other products not covered. Second, so-called "integrated mills" already produce all stages in an integrated process and would therefore be excluded if only the primary products were covered. Therefore, the final decision was to include some intermediate steel products, the so-called "precursors," with the exception of some ferro-alloys that are in short supply in the European Union (EU) (critical raw materials), such as ferro-silicon, ferro-molybdenum and ferro-vanadium. The line was drawn between intermediate and final products. For example, flat-rolled stainless steel is covered by the CBAM, but not the cars made from it. However, this may change in the future as the EU aims to have the same coverage as the EU Emissions Trading Scheme by 2035.

The product coverage and the greenhouse gas coverage by product group (CO_2, nitrous oxide [N_2O], perfluorocarbons [PFCs]) are defined in Annexes I and II of Regulation (EU) 2023/956 of the European Parliament and of the Council of 10 May 2023, establishing a carbon border adjustment mechanism.[1] A total of 560 products are covered at the 8-digit product level of the Combined Nomenclature, divided into six main groups and 15 subgroups.[2]

Table A1: Product List for EU Carbon Border Adjustment Mechanism

Products	Description	Harmonized System Codes
Cement	Calcined clay; cement clinker; cement; aluminous cement	25070080; 25231000; 25232100; 25232900; 25239000; 25233000.
Iron and steel	Sintered ore; pig iron; ferro-alloy: femn; ferro-alloy: fecr; ferro-alloy: feni; dri; crude steel; iron or steel products	26011200; 7201; 7205; 720210; 720240; 720260; 7203; 7206, 7207, 7218;7224; 7205, 7208, 7209, 7210, 7211, 7212, 7213, 7314, 7215, 7216, 7217, 7219, 7220, 7221, 7222,7223, 7225, 7226, 7227, 7228, 7229, 7301, 7301, 7303, 7304, 7305, 7306, 7307, 7308, 7309, 7310, 7311, 7318, 7326
Aluminum	Unwrought aluminum; aluminum products	7601; 7603, 7604, 7605, 7606, 7607, 7608, 7609, 7610, 7611, 7612, 7613, 7614, 7616
Fertilizers	Nitric acid; urea; ammonia; mixed fertilizers	2808 00 00; 3102 10;2814; 2834 21 00, 3102, 3105 - Except 3102 10 (Urea) and 3105 60 00
Electricity		2716
Hydrogen		Limited Trade

Source: Annex I and II of Regulation (EU) 2023/956 of the European Parliament and of the Council of 10 May 2023, establishing a carbon border adjustment mechanism.

Table A2: APEC List of Environmental Goods by Product Category and HS Line

#	Environmental Category	Number	Share (%)
1.	Environmentally preferable products	1	1.90
2.	Air pollution control	5	9.30
3.	Management of solid and hazardous waste and recycling systems	12	22.20
4.	Renewable energy production	15	27.80
5.	Wastewater management and potable water treatment	5	9.30
6.	Natural risk management	1	1.90
7.	Environmental monitoring analysis and assessment equipment	5	27.80
	Total Products	**54**	**100.00**

APEC = Asia-Pacific Economic Cooperation, HS = harmonized system.
Source: Asian Development Bank Compilation based on World Integrated System (WITS) database.

---

[1]   EUR-Lex. Regulation (EU) 2023/956 of the European Parliament and of the Council of 10 May 2023 establishing a carbon border adjustment mechanism. https://eur-lex.europa.eu/eli/reg/2023/956/oj.
[2]   See Table A1 in the Appendix for a full list of products covered by CBAM.

Table A3: Environmental Category in Combined List of Environmental Group

#	Environmental Category	HS 6 Digit Products	
		Number	Share (%)
1.	Air pollution control	12	4.84
2.	Cleaner or more resource-efficientt technologies and products	48	19.35
3.	Environmentally preferable products based on end use or disposal characteristics	6	2.42
4.	Heat and energy management	25	10.08
5.	Environmental monitoring, analysis, and assessment equipment	38	15.32
6.	Natural resources protection	3	1.21
7.	Noise and vibration abatement	3	1.21
8.	Renewable energy plant	54	21.77
9.	Management of solid and hazardous waste and recycling systems	25	10.08
10.	Clean up or remediation of soil and water	3	1.21
11.	Wastewater management and potable water treatment	31	12.50
	Total	**248**	**100.00**

HS = harmonized system.
Sources: Sauvage (2014); Asian Development Bank compilation based on World Integrated System (WITS) database.

Table A4: CPC Provisional Services Sectors Identified in Two Environmental Lists

	Services Sectors (as described in W/120)	APEC (2021)	GEA (2022)
1.	**Business Services**		
	A. Professional services	8	19
	C. Research and development services	1	5
	E. Rental/ leasing services without operators		8
	F. Other business services	7	13
3.	**Construction and Related Engineering Services**		
	A. General construction work for buildings		9
	B. General construction work for civil engineering	5	5
	C. Installation and assembly work	2	8
	E. Other	2	2
4.	**Distribution Services**		
	B. Wholesale trade services		3
6.	**Environment Services**		
	A. Sewage services	1	1
	B. Refuse disposal services	1	1
	C. Sanitation and similar services	1	1
	D. Other	4	4
7.	**Financial Services**		
	A. All insurance and insurance-related services		3
	B. Banking and other financial services		4
10.	**Recreational, Cultural, and Sporting Services**		
	C. Libraries, archives, museums, and other cultural activities	1	2
	D. Sporting and other recreational services	1	1
	Total	**34**	**76**

APEC = Asia-Pacific Economic Cooperation, CPC = central product classification, GEA = green economy agreement.
Note: The items are from the APEC environmentally-related services and the Singapore-Australia Green Economy Agreement.
Sources: APEC (2021) and Government of Singapore (n.d.).

Table A5: Product List for EU Deforestation Regulation—Relevant Commodities

Cattle

0102.21, 0102.29 Live cattle
ex. 0201 Meat of cattle, fresh or chilled
ex. 0202 Meat of cattle, frozen
ex. 0206.10 Edible offal of cattle, fresh or chilled
ex. 0206.22 Edible cattle livers, frozen
ex. 0206.29 Edible cattle offal (excluding tongues and livers), frozen
ex. 1602.50 Other prepared or preserved meat, meat offal, blood, of cattle

ex. 4101 Raw hides and skins of cattle (fresh, or salted, dried, limed, pickled or otherwise preserved, but not tanned, parchment-dressed or further prepared), whether or not dehaired or split
ex. 4104 Tanned or crust hides and skins of cattle, without hair on, whether or not split, but not further prepared
ex. 4107 Leather of cattle, further prepared after tanning or crusting, including parchment-dressed leather, without hair on, whether or not split, other than leather of heading 4114

Cocoa

1801 Cocoa beans, whole or broken, raw or roasted
1802 Cocoa shells, husks, skins and other cocoa waste
1803 Cocoa paste, whether or not defatted
1804 Cocoa butter, fat and oil

1805 Cocoa powder, not containing added sugar or other sweetening matter
1806 Chocolate and other food preparations containing cocoa

Coffee

0901 Coffee, whether or not roasted or decaffeinated; coffee husks and skins; coffee substitutes containing coffee in any proportion

Oil palm

1207.10 Palm nuts and kernels
1511 Palm oil and its fractions, whether or not refined, but not chemically modified
1513.21 Crude palm kernel and babassu oil and fractions thereof, whether or not refined, but not chemically modified
1513.29 Palm kernel and babassu oil and their fractions, whether or not refined, but not chemically modified (excluding crude oil)
2306.60 Oilcake and other solid residues of palm nuts or kernels, whether or not ground or in the form of pellets, resulting from the extraction of palm nut or kernel fats or oils
ex. 2905.45 Glycerol, with a purity of 95% or more (calculated on the weight of the dry product)

2915.70 Palmitic acid, stearic acid, their salts and esters
2915.90 Saturated acyclic monocarboxylic acids, their anhydrides, halides, peroxides and peroxyacids; their halogenated, sulphonated, nitrated or nitrosated derivatives (excluding formic acid, acetic acid, mono-, di- or trichloroacetic acids, propionic acid, butanoic acids, pentanoic acids, palmitic acid, stearic acid, their salts and esters, and acetic anhydride)
3823.11 Stearic acid, industrial
3823.12 Oleic acid, industrial
3823.19 Industrial monocarboxylic fatty acids; acid oils from refining (excluding stearic acid, oleic acid and tall oil fatty acids)
3823.70 Industrial fatty alcohols

Rubber

4001 Natural rubber, balata, gutta-percha, guayule, chicle and similar natural gums, in primary forms or in plates, sheets or strip
ex. 4005 Compounded rubber, unvulcanized, in primary forms or in plates, sheets or strip
ex. 4006 Unvulcanized rubber in other forms (e.g., rods, tubes and profile shapes) and articles (e.g., discs and rings)
ex. 4007 Vulcanized rubber thread and cord
ex. 4008 Plates, sheets, strips, rods and profile shapes, of vulcanized rubber other than hard rubber
ex. 4010 Conveyer or transmission belts or belting, of vulcanized rubber

ex. 4011 New pneumatic tires, of rubber
ex. 4012 Retreaded or used pneumatic tires of rubber; solid or cushion tires, tire treads and tire flaps, of rubber
ex. 4013 Inner tubes, of rubber
ex. 4015 Articles of apparel and clothing accessories (includin gloves, mittens and mitts), for all purposes, of vulcanized rubber other than hard rubber
ex. 4016 Other articles of vulcanized rubber other than hard rubber, not elsewhere specified in Chapter 40
ex. 4017 Hard rubber (e.g., ebonite) in all forms including waste and scrap; articles of hard rubber

continued on next page

Table A5 *continued*

Soya	
1201 Soya beans, whether or not broken 1208.10 Soya bean flour and meal 1507 Soya-bean oil and its fractions, whether or not refined, but not chemically modified	2304 Oilcake and other solid residues, whether or not ground or in the form of pellets, resulting from the extraction of soya-bean oil

Wood*	
4401 Fuel wood 4402 Wood charcoal 4403 Wood in the rough 4404 Hoopwood; split poles; piles of wood 4405 Wood wool; wood flour 4406 Railway or tramway sleepers (cross-ties) of wood 4407 Wood sawn or chipped lengthwise, sliced or peeled 4408 Sheets for veneering for plywood or for other similar laminated wood and other wood 4409 Wood continuously shaped along any of its edges 4410 Particle board, oriented strand board (OSB) and similar board of wood or other ligneous materials 4411 Fibreboard of wood or other ligneous materials 4412 Plywood, veneered panels and similar laminated wood 4413 Densified wood 4414 Wooden frames for paintings, photographs, mirrors or similar objects 4415 Packing cases, boxes, crates, drums and similar packings, of wood	4416 Casks, barrels, vats, tubs and other coopers' products and parts thereof, of wood, including staves 4417 Tools, tool bodies, tool handles, broom or brush bodies and handles, of wood 4418 Builders' joinery and carpentry of wood 4419 Tableware and kitchenware, of wood 4420 Wood marquetry and inlaid wood; caskets and cases for jewellery or cutlery, and similar articles, of wood 4421 Other articles of wood Pulp and paper of Chapters 47 and 48 of the Combined Nomenclature, with the exception of bamboo-based and recovered (waste and scrap) products ex. 49 Printed books, newspapers, pictures and other products of the printing industry, manuscripts, typescripts and plans, of paper ex. 9401 Seats (other than those of heading 9402), and parts thereof, of wood 9403.30 , 9403.40 , 9403.50 , 9403.60 and 9403.91 Wooden furniture, and parts thereof 9406.10 Prefabricated buildings of wood

Note: * Simplified HS codes description.
Source: EUR-Lex. Regulation (EU) 2023/1115 of 31 May 2023. https://eur-lex.europa.eu/eli/reg/2023/1115/oj (accessed 31 May 2024).

Bibliography

Acemoglu, D., P. Aghion, L. Bursztyn, and D. Hemous. 2012. The Environment and Directed Technical Change. *American Economic Review*. 102 (1). pp. 131–66. https://doi.org/10.1257/aer.102.1.131.

Ahman, M., M. Arens, and V. Vogl. 2022. International Cooperation for Decarbonizing Energy Intensive Industries: The Case for a Green Materials Club. In M. Jakob, ed. *Handbook on Trade Policy and Climate Change*. Edward Elgar.

Ai, L. and L. S. Gao. 2023. Firm-Level Risk of Climate Change: Evidence from Climate Disasters. *Global Finance Journal*. 55 (C). p. 100805.

Aldy, J. E. and W. A. Pizer. 2015. The Competitiveness Impacts of Climate Change Mitigation Policies. *Journal of the Association of Environmental and Resource Economists*. 2 (4). pp. 565–95. https://www.researchgate.net/publication/228268720_The_Competitiveness _Impacts_of_Climate_Change_Mitigation_Policies/link/09e4151150f49c1f28000000/ download?_tp=eyJjb250ZXh0Ijp7ImZpcnN0UGFnZSI6InB1YmxpY2F0aW9uIiwicGFnZSI6 InB1YmxpY2F0aW9uIn19.

Ali, S. et al. 2022. Exploring the Linkage between Export Diversification and Ecological Footprint: Evidence from Advanced Time Series Estimation Techniques. *Environmental Science and Pollution Research International*. 29 (25). pp. 38395–38409. https://www.researchgate.net/ publication/357661157_Exploring_the_linkage_between_export_diversification_and_ ecological_footprint_Evidence_from_advanced_time_series_estimation_techniques.

Angelucci, S., F. J. Hurtado-Albir, and A. Volpe. 2018. Supporting Global Initiatives on Climate Change: The EPO's 'Y02-Y04S' Tagging Scheme. *World Patent Information*. 54 (supplement). pp. S85-S92.

Asia-Pacific Economic Cooperation. 2018. Statement of the 6th Meeting of the APEC Ministers Responsible for Mining Meeting (MRM6). August 2018. https://www.apec.org/meeting-papers/sectoral-ministerial-meetings/mining/2018_mining.

———. 2021. Annex 2 - Reference List of Environmental and Environmentally Related Services. https://www.apec.org/meeting-papers/annual-ministerial-meetings/2021/2021-apec-ministerial-meeting/annex-2---reference-list-of-environmental-and-environmentally-related-services.

———. 2021. APEC Ministers Responsible for Trade Meeting Joint Statement 2021. https://www.apec.org/Meeting-Papers/Sectoral-Ministerial-Meetings/Trade/2021_MRT.

———. 2022. Time to Expand the APEC List of Environmental Goods. https://www.apec.org/press/blogs/2022/time-to-expand-the-apec-list-of-environmental-goods.

———. 2022. APEC Mining Activities. January 2022. https://www.apec.org/Groups/SOM-Steering-Committee-on-Economic-and-Technical-Cooperation/Mining.

Asian Development Bank (ADB). 2017. *Completion Report: Bangladesh, Bhutan, Nepal—South Subregional Economic Cooperation (SASEC) Trade Facilitation Program.*

———. 2022a. *Aid for Trade in Asia and the Pacific: Leveraging Trade and Digital Agreements for Sustainable Development.* https://dx.doi.org/10.22617/TCS220318-2.

———. 2022b. Completion Report: Pakistan: Trade and Competitiveness Program (Subprograms 1 and 2). https://www.adb.org/sites/default/files/project-documents/52049/52049-001-52049-003-pcr-en.pdf.

———. 2022c. Cambodia: Trade and Competitiveness Program, Subprogram 1. https://www.adb.org/projects/55255-001/main.

———. 2022d. *Completion Report: Trade and Competitiveness Program (Subprograms 1 and 2).*

———. 2022e. The Regional Comprehensive Economic Partnership Agreement: A New Paradigm in Asian Regional Cooperation?. http://dx.doi.org/10.22617/TCS220172-2.

———. 2023a. European Union Carbon Border Adjustment Mechanism: Economic Impact and Implications for Asia. *ADB Briefs.* No. 276.

———. 2023b. *Bangladesh: Trade and Global Value Chains.*

———. 2023c. *Asia Small and Medium-Sized Enterprise Monitor 2023: How Small Firms Can Contribute to Resilient Growth in the Pacific Post COVID-19 Pandemic.* https://www.adb.org/sites/default/files/publication/919641/asia-sme-monitor-2023.pdf.

———. 2023d. *Asian Economic Integration Report 2023: Trade, Investment and Climate Change in Asia and the Pacific.* https://aric.adb.org/pdf/aeir/AEIR2023_complete.pdf.

———. 2023e. Climate Adaptation Investment Planning. Brochure. https://www.adb.org/publications/climate-adaptation-investment-planning-brochure.

———. 2024. *Asian Economic Integration Report: Decarbonizing Global Value Chains.* https://aric.adb.org/pdf/aeir/AEIR2024_complete.pdf.

Bacchus, J. 2021. *Legal Issues with the European Carbon Border Adjustment Mechanism.* Briefing Paper No. 125. CATO Institute.

Baldwin, R. 2011. Trade and Industrialisation after Globalisation's 2nd Unbundling: How Building and Joining a Supply Chain Are Different and Why It Matters. *National Bureau for Economic Research Working Paper.* No. 17716. NBER.

Barrage, L. and W. Nordhaus 2024. Policies, Projections, and the Social Cost of Carbon: Results from the DICE-2023 Model. *Proceedings of the National Academy of Sciences.* 121 (13). p. e2312030121.

Bassi, A. M. and J. S. Yudken 2011. Climate Policy and Energy-Intensive Manufacturing: A Comprehensive Analysis of the Effectiveness of Cost Mitigation Provisions in the American Energy and Security Act of 2009. *Energy Policy.* 39 (9). pp. 4920–31. https://ideas.repec.org/a/eee/enepol/v39y2011i9p4920-4931.html.

Beaufils, T., H. Ward, M. Jakob, and L. Wenz. 2023. Assessing Different European Carbon Border Adjustment Mechanism Implementations and Their Impact on Trade Partners. *Communications Earth & Environment.* 4 (1). https://doi.org/10.1038/s43247-023-00788-4.

Bellora, C. and L. Fontagné. 2023. EU in Search of a Carbon Border Adjustment Mechanism. *Energy Economics.* 123. p. 106673. https://doi.org/10.1016/j.eneco.2023.106673.

Benincasa, E., F. Betz, and L. Gattini. 2024. How Do Firms Cope with Losses from Extreme Weather Events?. *Journal of Corporate Finance.* 84. p. 102508.

Bernard, A. B., J. B. Jensen, S. J. Redding, and P. K. Schott. 2007. *Firms in International Trade.*

Birkbeck, C. D. 2021. *Greening International Trade: Pathways Forward.* geneva.fes.de/fileadmin/user_upload/documents/2021/2021_11_Greening_Aid_for_Trade.pdf.

Blondeel, M., M. J. Bradshaw, G. Bridge, and C. Kuzemko. 2021. The Geopolitics of Energy System Transformation: A Review. *Geography Compass.* 15 (7). https://compass.onlinelibrary.wiley.com/doi/10.1111/gec3.12580.

Böhringer, C., A. Müller, and J. Schneider. 2015. Carbon Tariffs Revisited. *Journal of the Association of Environmental and Resource Economists.* 2 (4). pp. 629–72. https://doi.org/10.1086/683607.

Böhringer, C., C. Fischer, and K. E. Rosendahl. 2010. The Global Effects of Subglobal Climate Policies. *B.E. Journal of Economic Analysis and Policy.* 10 (2). https://doi.org/10.2202/1935-1682.2583.

Böhringer, C., C. Fischer, K. E. Rosendahl, and T. F. Rutherford. 2022. Potential Impacts and Challenges of Border Carbon Adjustments. *Nature Climate Change.* 12 (1). pp. 22–29. https://doi.org/10.1038/s41558-021-01250-z.

Böhringer, C., E. J. Balistreri, and T. F. Rutherford. 2012. The Role of Border Carbon Adjustment in Unilateral Climate Policy: Overview of an Energy Modeling Forum Study (EMF 29). *Energy Economics*. 34 (s2). pp. S97–S110. https://doi.org/10.1016/j.eneco.2012.10.003.

Böhringer, C., J. C. Carbone, and T. F. Rutherford. 2016. The Strategic Value of Carbon Tariffs. *American Economic Journal: Economic Policy*. 8 (1). pp. 28–51. https://doi.org/10.1257/pol.20130327.

———. 2018. Embodied Carbon Tariffs. *Scandinavian Journal of Economics*. 120 (1). pp. 183–210.

Boyd, R. and A. Ufimtseva. 2021. Facilitating Peaceful Rise: The Increasing Role of Geopolitics and Domestic Legitimacy in China's Energy Policy. *Energy Policy*. 158 (November). p. 112532. https://doi.org/10.1016/j.enpol.2021.112532.

Brandi, C., J-F. Morin, and F. Stender. 2022. Do Trade Agreements Call for Side-Payments?. *Journal of Environment and Development*. 3 (2). pp. 111–138.

Brandi, C., J. Schwab, A. Berger, and J. F. Morin. 2020. Do Environmental Provisions in Trade Agreements Make Exports from Developing Countries Greener?. *World Development*. 129 (May).

Branger, F. and P. Quirion. 2014. Would Border Carbon Adjustments Prevent Carbon Leakage and Heavy Industry Competitiveness Losses? Insights from a Meta-Analysis of Recent Economic Studies. *Ecological Economics*. 99 (March). pp. 29–39. https://doi.org/10.1016/j.ecolecon.2013.12.010.

Bristow, G. 2005. Everyone's a 'Winner': Problematising the Discourse of Regional Competitiveness. *Journal of Economic Geography*. 5 (3). pp. 285–304.

Calel, R. and A. Dechezleprêtre. 2016. Environmental Policy and Directed Technological Change: Evidence from the European Carbon Market. *Review of Economics and Statistics*. 98 (1). pp. 173–91. https://doi.org/10.1162/REST_a_00470.

Carbon Pricing Leadership Coalition. 2017. Report of the High-Level Commission on Carbon Prices. https://www.carbonpricingleadership.org/report-of-the-highlevel-commission-on-carbon-prices/.

Carbone, J. C. and N. Rivers. 2017. The Impacts of Unilateral Climate Policy on Competitiveness: Evidence From Computable General Equilibrium Models. *Review of Environmental Economics and Policy*. 11 (1). pp. 24–42. https://doi.org/10.1093/reep/rew025.

Caron, J. 2022. Empirical Evidence and Projections of Carbon Leakage: Some, but Not Too Much, Probably. In M. Jakob, ed. *Handbook on Trade Policy and Climate Change, Elgar Handbooks in Energy, the Environment and Climate Change*.

Chepeliev, M., A. Aguiar, T. Farole, A. Liverani, and D. van der Mensbrugghe. 2022. EU Green Deal and Circular Economy Transition: Impacts and Interactions. Paper presented at the 25th Annual Conference on Global Economic Analysis (Virtual Conference).

Chepeliev, M. and E. Corong. 2022. Revisiting the Environmental Bias of Trade Policies Based on an Environmentally Extended GTAP MRIO Data Base. Center for Global Trade Analysis, Purdue University.

Cherniwchan, J. and M. S. Taylor. 2022. International Trade and the Environment: Three Remaining Empirical Challenges. *NBER Working Paper*. No. 30020. National Bureau of Economic Research.

Clarke, L., Y.-M. Wei, A. De La Vega Navarro, A. Garg, A.N. Hahmann, S. Khennas, I.M.L. Azevedo, A. Löschel, A.K. Singh, L. Steg, G. Strbac, K. Wada, 2022: Energy Systems. In IPCC, ed. Climate Change 2022: Mitigation of Climate Change. Contribution of Working Group III to the Sixth Assessment Report of the Intergovernmental Panel on Climate Change [P.R. Shukla, J. Skea, R. Slade, A. Al Khourdajie, R. van Diemen, D. McCollum, M. Pathak, S. Some, P. Vyas, R. Fradera, M. Belkacemi, A. Hasija, G. Lisboa, S. Luz, J. Malley, (eds.)]. doi: 10.1017/9781009157926.008.

Climate Policy Radar. 2023. Climate Change Laws of the World. https://climate-laws.org/.

Climate Resource. 2024. NDC Factsheets. https://www.climate-resource.com/tools/ndcs.

Comtrade. 2024. UN Comtrade Database. https://comtradeplus.un.org/.

Cramton, P., D. J. C. MacKay, A. Ockenfels, and S. Stoft. 2017. *Global Carbon Pricing. The Path to Climate Cooperation*. MIT Press. https://mitpress.mit.edu/9780262036269/global-carbonpricing/.

Crivelli, P., S. Inama, and G. Pascua. 2023. For Cambodia, Celebration and New Trade Challenges. ADB blog. No. 31. https://blogs.adb.org/blog/cambodia-celebration-and-new-trade-challenges.

Crivelli, P. Diversifying Global Value Chains [Unpublished proposal].

Crivelli, P., S. Inama, and G. Pascua. 2023. For Cambodia, Celebration and New Trade Challenges. ADB blog. No. 31. https://blogs.adb.org/blog/cambodia-celebration-and-new-trade-challenges.

Crivelli, P., J. Marand, and G. Pascua. 2022. *Liberalizing Services Trade in the Regional Comprehensive Economic Partnership: Status and Ways Forward*. ADB Briefs. No. 237. https://dx.doi.org/10.22617/BRF220573-2.

Davis, S. J. et al. 2018. Net-Zero Emissions Energy Systems. *Science*. 360 (6396). p. eaas9793. https://doi.org/10.1126/science.aas9793.

Dechezleprêtre, A. and M. Sato. 2017. The Impacts of Environmental Regulations on Competitiveness. *Review of Environmental Economics and Policy*. 11 (2). pp. 183–206. https://doi.org/10.1093/reep/rex013.

Delera, M. and N. Foster-McGregor. 2020. On PTAs and Bilateral Trade: IS GVC Trade Sensitive to the Breadth of Trade Policy Cooperation? *Economies*. 8 (4). p. 84.

Delera, M. and N. Foster-McGregor. 2023. Revisiting International Knowledge Spillovers: The Role of GVCs. *Industrial and Corporate Change*. 32 (5). pp. 1163–1191.

Do, T. N., P. Burke, K. G. H. Baldwin, and C. T. Nguyen. 2020. Underlying Drivers and Barriers for Solar Photovoltaics Diffusion: The Case of Vietnam. *Energy Policy*. 144. Article ID: 111561. https://doi.org/10.1016/j.enpol.2020.111561.

Dröge, S. 2009. *Tackling Leakage in a World of Unequal Carbon Prices*. Climate Strategies.

Eaton, J. and S. Kortum. 1996. Trade in Ideas: Patenting and Productivity in the OECD. *Journal of International Economics*. 40 (3–4). pp. 251–278.

European Commission. 2021. *Impact Assessment Report: Proposal for a Regulation of the European Parliament and of the Council Establishing a Carbon Border Adjustment Mechanism*. European Commission Staff Working Document.

———. 2023a. Commission Implementing Regulation (EU) 2023/1773 of 17 August 2023 laying down the rules for the application of Regulation (EU) 2023/956 of the European Parliament and of the Council as regards reporting obligations for the purposes of the carbon border adjustment mechanism during the transitional period (Text with EEA relevance).

———. 2023b. Guidance Document on CBAM Implementation for Importers of Goods into the EU. Directorate-General Taxation and Customs Union, Indirect Taxation and Tax Administration, CBAM, Energy and Green Taxation. 13 December.

———. 2024. Carbon Border Adjustment Mechanism: Questions and Answers. 28 February 2024.

European Parliament. 2020. Economic Assessment of Carbon Leakage and Carbon Border Adjustment. Briefing. Directorate-General for External Policies.

Evdokia, M. and S. Rubínová. 2021. Sustainability Impact Assessments of Free Trade Agreements: A Critical Review. *OECD Trade Policy Papers*. No. 255.

Falcao, T. 2020. Toward Carbon Tax Internationalism: The EU Border Carbon Adjustment Proposal. *Tax Notes International*. 98 (9).

Global Carbon Project. 2023. The Latest GCB Data. https://globalcarbonbudgetdata.org/latest-data.html.

Government of Singapore. 2022. Singapore-Australia Green Economy Agreement (SAGEA). https://www.gea.gov.sg/SAGEA/.

———. n.d. Singapore-Australia Green Economy Agreement, Annex B 1.2: Environmental Services List. https://file.go.gov.sg/sagea-environmental-services-list.pdf.

Grubb, M., N. D. Jordan, E. Hertwich, K. Neuhoff, K. Das, K. R. Bandyopadhyay, H. van Asselt, M. Sato, R. Wang, W. A. Pizer, and H. Oh. 2022. Carbon Leakage, Consumption, and Trade. *Annual Review of Environment and Resources* 47. pp. 753–795. https://doi.org/10.1146/annurev-environ-120820-053625.

Gugler, K., F. Szücs, and T. Wiedenhofer. 2024. Environmental Policies and Directed Technological Change. *Journal of Environmental Economics and Management.* 124 (March). 102916. https://doi.org/10.1016/j.jeem.2023.102916.

Haider, K. and K. Anis. 2015. Heat Wave Death Toll Rises to 2,000 in Pakistan's Financial Hub. *Bloomberg* [online]. 24 June.

Hakobyan, S., S. Meleshchuk, and R. Zymek. 2023. Divided We Fall: Differential Exposure to Geopolitical Fragmentation in Trade. *IMF Working Paper.* No. 2023/270. International Monetary Fund.

Hofmann, C., A. Osnago, and M. Ruta. 2017. Horizontal Depth: A New Database on the Content of Preferential Trade Agreements. *World Bank Policy Research Working Paper.* No. 7981. The World Bank.

Intergovernmental Panel on Climate Change (IPCC). 2018. Summary for Policymakers. In V. Masson-Delmotte et al., eds. *An IPCC Special Report on the Impacts of Global Warming of 1.5C Above Pre-Industrial Levels and Related Global Greenhouse Gas Emission Pathways, in the Context of Strengthening the Global Response to the Threat of Climate Change, Sustainable Development, and Efforts to Eradicate Poverty.* Geneva: World Meteorological Organization. p. 32.

———. 2022. Climate Change 2022: Mitigation of Climate Change. Working Group III Contribution to the IPCC Sixth Assessment Report.

International Energy Agency (IEA). 2021. Net Zero by 2050: A Roadmap for the Global Energy Sector. Paris. https://www.iea.org/reports/net-zero-by-2050.

———. 2022. *Special Report on Solar PV Global Supply Chains.* Paris. https://www.iea.org/reports/solar-pv-global-supply-chains.

———. 2023. *Critical Minerals Market Review 2023.* Paris: IEA. https://www.iea.org/reports/critical-minerals-market-review-2023.

International Institute for Sustainable Development (IISD). 2020. Trading Services for a Circular Economy. https://www.iisd.org/publications/trading-services-circular-economy.

International Labour Organization (ILO). 2017. *World Social Protection Report 2017–19: Universal Social Protection to Achieve the Sustainable Development Goals.*

————. 2019. Working on a Warmer Planet: The Effect of Heat Stress on Productivity and Decent Work. https://www.ilo.org/publications/major-publications/working-warmer-planet-effect-heat-stress-productivity-and-decent-work.

International Monetary Fund. 2022 (IMF). Global Trade and Value Chains During the Pandemic. *World Economic Outlook April 2022: War Sets Back the Global Recovery.* https://www.elibrary.imf.org/display/book/9781616359423/9781616359423.xml.

————. 2023. IMF Fossil Fuel Subsidies Data: 2023 Update. https://www.imf.org/en/Topics/climate-change/energysubsidies#Energy%20Subsidies.

International Trade Centre. 2023. SME Competitiveness Outlook 2023: Small Businesses in Fragility: From Survival to Growth. https://intracen.org/resources/publications/sme-competitiveness-outlook-2023-small-businesses-in-fragility-from-survival.

Iraldo, F., F. Testa, M. Melis, and M. Frey. 2011. A Literature Review on the Links between Environmental Regulation and Competitiveness. *Environmental Policy and Governance.* 21 (3). pp. 210–22. https://doi.org/10.1002/eet.568.

Jakob, M., H. Ward, and J. C. Steckel. 2021. Sharing Responsibility for Trade-Related Emissions Based on Economic Benefits. *Global Environmental Change.* 66 (January). p. 102207. https://doi.org/10.1016/j.gloenvcha.2020.102207.

Jakob, M. et al. 2022. How Trade Policy Can Support the Climate Agenda. *Science.* 376 (6600). pp. 1401–3. https://doi.org/10.1126/science.abo4207.

Jakob, M. 2021a. Why Carbon Leakage Matters and What Can Be Done against It. *One Earth.* 4 (5). pp. 609–14. https://doi.org/10.1016/j.oneear.2021.04.010.

Jakob, M. 2021b. Climate Policy and International Trade – A Critical Appraisal of the Literature. *Energy Policy.* 156 (September). p. 112399. https://doi.org/10.1016/j.enpol.2021.112399.

Jitsutthiphakorn, U. 2021. Innovation, Firm Productivity, and Export Survival: Firm-Level Evidence from ASEAN Developing Countries. *Journal of Economic Structures.* 10 (1). p.22.

Kaufman, N., S. Saha, and C. Bataille. 2023. Green Trade Tensios: Green Industrial Policy Will Drive Decarbonization, But at What Cost to Trade?. https://www.imf.org/en/Publications/fandd/issues/2023/06/green-trade-tensions-kaufman-saha-bataille.

Koch, N. and H. Basse Mama. 2019. Does the EU Emissions Trading System Induce Investment Leakage? Evidence from German Multinational Firms. *Energy Economics.* 81 (June). pp. 479–92. https://doi.org/10.1016/j.eneco.2019.04.018.

Kortum, S. and D. A. Weisbach. 2023. Optimal Unilateral Carbon Policy. Working Paper. https://www.law.nyu.edu/sites/default/files/Optimal%20Unilateral%20Carbon%20Policy.pdf.

Kotz, M., A. Levermann, and L. Wenz. 2024. The Economic Commitment of Climate Change. *Nature*. 628 (8008). pp. 551–57. https://doi.org/10.1038/s41586-024-07219-0.

Kuik, O. and M. Hofkes. 2010. Border Adjustment for European Emissions Trading: Competitiveness and Carbon Leakage. *Energy Policy*. 38 (4). pp. 1741–48. https://doi.org/10.1016/j.enpol.2009.11.048.

Leiserowitz, A., J. Carman, N. Buttermore, L. Neyens, S. Rosenthal, J. Marlon, J. Schneider, and K. Mulcahy. 2022. International Public Opinion on Climate Change. https://climatecommunication.yale.edu/publications/international-public-opinion-on-climate-change-2022/.

Letchumanan, R. and F. Kodama. 2000. Reconciling the Conflict between the 'Pollution-Haven' Hypothesis and an Emerging Trajectory of International Technology Transfer. *Research Policy*. 29 (1). pp. 59–79. https://doi.org/10.1016/S0048-7333(99)00033-5.

Mao, X., H. Liu, J. Gui and P. Wang. 2023. Toward Inclusive List-Making for Trade Liberalization in Environmental Goods to Reduce Carbon Emissions. *Geography and Sustainability*. 4 (3). pp. 200-212.

Martínez-Zarzoso, I. and S. Chelala. 2021. Trade Agreements and International Technology Transfer. *Review of World Economics*. 157. pp. 631–655.

Mattoo, A., N. Rocha, and M. Ruta. 2020. *Handbook of Deep Trade Agreements*. World Bank.

Mehling, M. A., H. van Asselt, K. Das, S. Droege, and C. Verkuijl. 2019. Designing Border Carbon Adjustments for Enhanced Climate Action. *American Journal of International Law*. 113 (3). pp. 433–81. https://doi.org/10.1017/ajil.2019.22.

Ministry of Economy, Republic of Fiji. 2021. Fiji National Climate Change Policy. Briefing Note. https://fijiclimatechangeportal.gov.fj/wp-content/uploads/2022/01/Brief__Fiji_National_Climate_Change_Policy.pdf.

Moïsé, E. and S. Rubínová. 2021. Sustainability Impact Assessments of Free Trade Agreements: A Critical Review. *OECD Trade Policy Papers*. No. 255. OECD Publishing.

Monkelbaan, J., J. Keane, and R. Kaukab. n.d. Greening Aid for Trade. Working Paper No. 4 in Trade and Environmental Sustainability Series.

Mortha, A. and T. H. Arimura. 2024. Effect of a European Carbon Border Adjustment Mechanism on Asia and the Pacific. *Centre for Economic Policy Research*. 27 February.

Mortha, A., T. H. Arimura, S. Takeda, and T. Chesnokova. 2023. Effect of a European Carbon Border Adjustment Mechanism on the APAC Region: A Structural Gravity Analysis. RIETI Discussion Paper Series. No. 23-E-058.

National Board of Trade. 2020. Border Carbon Adjustments: An Analysis of Trade Related Aspects and the Way Forward.

Net Zero Tracker. 2024. Data Explorer. https://zerotracker.net/#data-explorer.

Nordström, H. 2023. Does the Risk of Carbon Leakage Justify the CBAM. Rapport 2023:01. Swedish Agency for Growth Policy Analysis.

————. 2024. Lessons from the First Reporting Period of the EU's Carbon Border Adjustment Mechanism. Aid for Trade report background paper. ADB.

OECD and Statistical Office of the European Communities. 1999. *The Environmental Goods and Services Industry: Manual for Data Collection and Analysis*. OECD Publishing.

Organisation for Economic Co-operation and Development (OECD). 2012. *Green Growth and Developing Countries: A Summary for Policymakers*.

————. 2017. *Trade in Services Related to the Environment*. https://one.oecd.org/document/COM/TAD/ENV/JWPTE(2015)61/FINAL/En/pdf.

————. 2021. *G20/OECD/International Labour Organization Report on MSMEs in the Global Economy*. https://www.oecd.org/g20/topics/inclusive-growth/G20-EWG-ILO-OECD-MSME-Report-FINAL.pdf.

————. 2023. *The Observatory of Economic Complexity*. https://oec.world/en.

Perdana, S. and M. Vielle. 2022. Making the EU Carbon Border Adjustment Mechanism Acceptable and Climate Friendly for Least Developed Countries. *Energy Policy*. 170. p. 113245. https://doi.org/10.1016/j.enpol.2022.113245.

Porter, M. E. and C. Van Der Linde. 1995. Toward a New Conception of the Environment-Competitiveness Relationship. *Journal of Economic Perspectives*. 9 (4). pp. 97–118. https://doi.org/10.1257/jep.9.4.97.

Pörtner, H.-O. et al., eds. 2022. *Climate Change 2022: Impacts, Adaptation and Vulnerability. Contribution of Working Group II to the Sixth Assessment Report of the Intergovernmental Panel on Climate Change*. IPCC.

Quint, D. 2008. Patent Pools. In M. Vernengo, E. P. Caldentey, and B. J. Rosser Jr. *The New Palgrave Dictionary of Economics*. 2nd edition. Palgrave Macmillan.

Sato, M. and A. Dechezleprêtre. 2015. Asymmetric Industrial Energy Prices and International Trade. *Energy Economics*. 52 (December). pp. S130–41. https://doi.org/10.1016/j.eneco.2015.08.020.

Sauvage, J. 2014. The Stringency of Environmental Regulations and Trade in Environmental Goods. *OECD Trade and Environment Working Papers*. No. 2014/03. http://dx.doi.org/10.1787/5jxrjn7xsnmq-en.

Schinko, T., B. Bednar-Friedl, K. W. Steininger, and W. D. Grossmann. 2014. Switching to Carbon-Free Production Processes: Implications for Carbon Leakage and Border Carbon Adjustment. *Energy Policy*. 67 (April). pp. 818–31. https://doi.org/10.1016/j.enpol.2013.11.077.

Shahzad, U. et al. 2020. Export Product Diversification and CO_2 Emissions: Contextual evidences from Developing and Developed Economies. *Journal of Cleaner Production*. 276. https://doi.org/10.1016/j.jclepro.2020.124146.

Steenblick, R. 2005. Environmental Goods: A Comparison of the APEC and OECD Lists. *OECD Trade and Environmental Working Paper*. No. 2005–04.

Takeda, S. and T. H. Arimura. 2024. A Computable General Equilibrium Analysis of the EU CBAM for the Japanese Economy. *Japan and the World Economy*. 70 (June). p. 101242. https://doi.org/10.1016/j.japwor.2024.101242.

Tong, D., Q. Zhang, Y. Zheng, K. Caldeira, C. Shearer, C. Hong, Y. Qin, and S. J. Davis. 2019. Committed Emissions from Existing Energy Infrastructure Jeopardize 1.5 °C Climate Target. *Nature*. 572 (7769). pp. 373–77. https://doi.org/10.1038/s41586-019-1364-3.

United Nations Conference on Trade and Development (UNCTAD). 2006. Preserving Flexibility in IIAs: The Use of Reservations. https://www.un-ilibrary.org/content/books/9789211555462/read.

———. 2021. *A European Union Carbon Border Adjustment Mechanism: Implications for Developing Countries*.

———. 2023. Official International Assistance Insufficient to Reach 2030 Agenda. https://sdgpulse.unctad.org/development-financing/.

United Nations Environment Programme (UNEP). 2019. Small Island Developing States Waste Management Outlook, online at https://www.unep.org/ietc/node/44.

———. 2020. Aid for Trade: A Vehicle to Green Trade and Build Climate Resilience. Issue Brief. April. https://wedocs.unep.org/bitstream/handle/20.500.11822/32204/AfT.pdf?sequence=1.

Vekasi, K. 2023. Critical Minerals Trade and the Green Energy Transition. The Role of APEC. National Bureau of Asian Research. Commentary from APEC. June. https://www.nbr.org/publication/critical-minerals-trade-and-the-green-energy-transition-the-role-of-apec/.

Verde, S. 2020. The Impact of the EU Emissions Trading System on Competitiveness and Carbon Leakage: The Econometric Evidence. *Journal of Economic Surveys*. 34 (2). pp. 320–343.

Vu, H. V., M. Holmes, T. Q. Tran, and S. Lim. 2016. Firm Exporting and Productivity: What If Productivity Is No Longer a Black Box. *Baltic Journal of Economics*. 16 (2). pp. 95–113.

Wang, M., X. Mao, Y. Xing, J. Lu, P. Song, Z. Liu, Z. Guo, K. Tu and E. Zusman. 2021. Breaking Down Barriers on PV Trade Will Facilitate Global Carbon Mitigation. *Nature Communications*. 12. pp. 1–16.

Wang, Z., S.J. Wei, X. Yu, and K. Zhu. 2017. Measures of Participation in Global Value Chains and Global Business Cycles. *National Bureau of Economic Research Working Paper*. No. 23222. NBER.

Ward, H., J. C. Steckel, and M. Jakob. 2019. How Global Climate Policy Could Affect Competitiveness. *Energy Economics*. 84 (October). p. 104549. https://doi.org/10.1016/j.eneco.2019.104549.

Witecka, W., J. Somers, K. Reimann, N. Wagner, O. Zelt, A. Julich, S. Clemens, and M. Åhman. 2024. Low-Carbon Technologies for the Global Steel Transformation. Agora Energiewende. https://portal.research.lu.se/en/publications/low-carbon-technologies-for-the-global-steel-transformation.

World Bank. 2022. *State and Trends of Carbon Pricing 2022*.

———. 2024a. Carbon Pricing Dashboard. https://carbonpricingdashboard.worldbank.org/.

———. 2024b. World Development Indicators. https://databank.worldbank.org/reports.aspx?source=World-Development-Indicators.

World Intellectual Property Organization (WIPO). 2009. *WIPO Magazine*.

World Trade Organization (WTO). 1994a. Marrakesh Agreement Establishing the World Trade Organization. https://www.wto.org/english/docs_e/legal_e/04-wto_e.htm.

———. 1994b. Environment Features in Uruguay Round Results and Emerges as Priority Issue in Post-Uruguay Round Work of GATT. https://www.wto.org/gatt_docs/English/SULPDF/91760098.pdf.

———. 1994c. Relevant WTO Provisions: Text of 1994 Decision. https://www.wto.org/english/tratop_e/envir_e/issu5_e.htm.

———. 1994d. Decision on Trade in Services and the Environment. https://www.wto.org/english/tratop_e/serv_e/15-env_e.htm.

———. 2001. DOHA WTO Ministerial 2001: Ministerial Declaration. https://www.wto.org/english/thewto_e/minist_e/min01_e/mindecl_e.htm.

———. 2009. *Communication under paragraph 31 (III) of the Doha Ministerial Declaration*. JOB(09)/132. Committee on Trade and Environment Special Session.

———. 2016. *World Trade Report 2016: Levelling the Trading Field for SMEs.* https://www.wto.org/english/res_e/booksp_e/wtr16-4_e.pdf.

———. 2019. Trade and Climate Change. Information Brief. No. 1. https://www.wto.org/english/news_e/news21_e/clim_03nov21-1_e.pdf.

———. 2022a. World Trade Report 2022: Climate Change and International Trade. https://www.wto.org/english/res_e/publications_e/wtr22_e.htm.

———. 2022b. *World Trade Report: Climate Change and International Trade.*

Zhong, J. and J. Pei. 2022. Beggar Thy Neighbor? On the Competitiveness and Welfare Impacts of the EU's Proposed Carbon Border Adjustment Mechanism. *Energy Policy.* 162 (March). p. 112802. https://doi.org/10.1016/j.enpol.2022.112802.

———. 2024. Carbon Border Adjustment Mechanism: A Systematic Literature Review of the Latest Developments. *Climate Policy.* 24 (2). pp. 228–42. https://doi.org/10.1080/14693062.2023.2190074.

Zhuawu C. and K. Powell. 2022. *Reigniting Old Flames: The Liberalisation of Trade in Environmental Goods and Services.* https://www.thecommonwealth-ilibrary.org/index.php/comsec/catalog/download/957/953/8199?inline=1.

www.ingramcontent.com/pod-product-compliance
Lightning Source LLC
Chambersburg PA
CBHW040250290326
41929CB00058B/3499